Lessons From My Grandfather

WISDOM FOR SUCCESS IN BUSINESS AND LIFE
2023 EDITION

Marc Charles Demetriou

www.GrandfatherLessons.com

Copyright © 2023, Marc C. Demetriou and Success House Publishing
Cover design by Julia McMinn Evans
Interior book design by Sarah Clarehart

All rights and international rights reserved. No part of this product, including but not limited to any portion thereof may be reproduced, distributed, or transmitted in any form or by any means, including photocopying, recording, or other electronic or mechanical methods, nor may it be stored in a retrieval system, transmitted or otherwise copied for public or private use, without the prior written permission of the publisher, except "fair use" of brief quotations embodied in critical reviews and certain other noncommercial uses permitted by copyright law. For permission requests, write to the publisher, addressed "Attention: Permissions Coordinator," at the e-mail address above.

The intent of the author is only to offer general information to help you in your quest for greater personal and professional success. Buyers and readers agree that the publisher and/or the author are not engaged to render any type of medical, psychological, legal, or any other kind of professional advice. If you believe you need assistance, please consult a professional. Neither the publisher nor the individual author shall be liable for any physical, psychological, emotional, financial, or commercial damages, including, but not limited to special, incidental, consequential or other damages. You are responsible for your own choices, actions, and results.

2023
Paperback Edition ISBN 979-8-9862590-9-3
Library of Congress Control Number 2023904365

1. Self-Help 2. Business Skills 3. Priceless Wisdom

For more information, visit www.grandfatherlessons.com

Acclaim for
Lessons From My Grandfather

"Not all of us are fortunate enough to grow up with a mentor who can provide us with the wisdom, insight, and life lessons that author Marc Demetriou obtained from his grandfather, whose mentoring supported him to the successful life he experiences today. For anyone without such a formidable source of ageless wisdom, Lessons From My Grandfather provides its readers with access to the same advice and life lessons. In sharing his grandfather's sage experience and viewpoint, Demetriou has provided a significant gift to his readers and the larger world." — **Brian Smith, UGG Founder**

"Reading Lessons From My Grandfather was a thrill because it is so rare to encounter a book with this much potential to change lives for the better. As a lifelong entrepreneur, what resonated with me most was how the wisdom handed down from Marc Demetriou's immigrant grandfather, Charlie, who came through Ellis Island in 1929, maps to the success formulas essential to starting a career or new business today. It's all here! I consider this inspiring book to be essential reading for anyone with dreams of success in life, as well as in business." — **Alec Stern, Co-Founder, Constant Contact, "America's Startup Success Expert"**

"Marc Demetriou has written a superb success guide unlike any other. Based on fifteen universal principles, Lessons From My Grandfather will help you achieve the success you deserve in life and business." — **Barbara Corcoran Founder, The Corcoran Group and investor on ABC's Emmy Award-winning show,** *Shark Tank*

"I encourage you to read Marc Demetriou's new book, Lessons from My Grandfather. One of the best ways to learn something is by associating yourself with someone who knows more than you do. By reading this book, you will be able to associate yourself with someone who truly knows the meaning of success." — **Don Green, CEO and Executive Director of the Napoleon Hill Foundation**

"If Napoleon Hill had found out about Marc's grandfather, he probably would have some of grandfather's life episodes and experiences in his works. Marc has turned his grandfather's ancient wisdom into a practical and easy to understand guide for success for new millennium. This epic work brings a new hope of giving you another way of looking at your world in which you can have, be and do anything you want, irrespective of your age, gender or race." — **Satish C. Verma, President & CEO, Think and Grow Rich Institute**

"Your book is a powerful tribute to your grandfather and to all of us who were influenced by our grandparents who came from another country to this great country for a better life " — **Steve Adubato, host, "Caucus NJ"**

"This book is about dreams, hope, and happiness fulfilled through courage, perseverance, humility, and an attitude that anyone reaching for success will treasure. Charlie, the immigrant, who received no public recognition or accolades in his lifetime, has a greater monument in a book by his grateful and adoring grandson who shares with all of us Charlie's profound lessons for a great and successful life." — **Anthony Scardino, Jr., New Jersey State Senator (ret)**

"Marc has reflected on his teachings of his grandfather and others close to him to embody witticism, lessons, and inspiration in dealing with all of the challenges and opportunities in front of anyone seeking success and fulfillment. Lessons From My Grandfather will help build a bridge toward personal and professional enlightenment." — **Chris Martin, President, Chief Executive Officer and Chairman of The Provident Bank; President, Chief Executive Officer and Chairman of Provident Financial Services Inc.**

Acclaim for *Lessons's From My Grandfather*

"Marc Demetriou has written a wonderful, insightful story that will allow anyone to improve his or her own life. I particularly love the connection to the sage wisdom of our grandfathers. This brought back fond memories of my own grandfather giving me his advice. We could all use such wisdom in these fast-paced, instant-gratification times. This enjoyable book is a wonderful way to reflect on how our grandparents might approach the decisions and choices of today."
— Don A. Holbrook, author, *The Next America: How to Survive and Thrive in Today's Unpredictable Economy*

"*Lessons From My Grandfather* takes you on an inspirational journey from one generation of success to another. Marc has captured true gems from his grandfather's history, along with his own personal experiences and concepts from modern-day leaders in business and philosophy, to create a roadmap to help you create your own vision of success." — Daniel A. Prisciotta, CFP®, CPA/PFS, ChFC®, CBEC®, President, PrisCo Financial

"I've been business partners with Marc on a few different ventures over the last twenty years. He's one of the most energetic and insightful business minds I've ever worked with. This book shares some unique principles for his secrets to success. Thanks Marc!" — Joe Occhiogrosso best-selling author, *A Story About, "I Will Never Do Network Marketing"*

"Marc's personal story alone makes him someone to listen to when he explains how to achieve success in any field. When he adds in the wisdom of his grandfather, Charlie, you have two great role models to provide real-world lessons about the nuts and bolts that are the keys for all high-achievers. I know something about that, having interviewed many of America's top CEOs. I urge you to put this book at the top of your reading list now." — Scott S. Smith author, *Extraordinary People: Real Life Lessons on What It Takes to Achieve Success*

"Marc Demetriou had the good fortune and foresight to preserve the wisdom passed along by his grandfather, a man who came from humble beginnings as an immigrant to the US in the early 20th century and achieved great success in many ways. Demetriou masterfully weaves together his grandfather's words with all that he has learned in his own life and career to produce a special book filled with easy-to-apply suggestions." — David J. Singer, author of *Six Simple Rules for a Better Life*

"While ostensibly written for an adult readership, *Lessons From My Grandfather* also has tremendous value for high school and college students. A compelling read, the book has great potential for helping young individuals find their way along the complex road that leads to adulthood. Simultaneously aspirational and inspirational, throughout the text Mr. Demetriou keeps both feet on the ground by offering readers a finely balanced mixture of 'big picture' strategies with sound practical advice for achieving personal success. I thoroughly enjoyed this book and would not hesitate to recommend it to my professional educator colleagues for use in their own classrooms." — David C. Verducci, Ph.D., Superintendent of Schools, retired

"How do you measure a successful life, and what are the secrets to achieving it? Marc Demetriou's grandfather, Charlie, provided a blueprint for success that is still profoundly relevant for today and the years to come. There's wisdom for everybody in this essential book." — Tom Corley, three-time bestselling author of *Rich Habits, Rich Kids and Change Your Habits Change Your Life*

"Charlie Pistis was a self-made man who came to this country with nothing and achieved great success. His inspirational story inspired author and grandson Marc Demetriou to achieve his own success. Through Marc's book, he will help you build recognition, clarity, and vision on your own road to fulfillment."
— Henry Fein, attorney, Fein, Such, Kahn & Shepard, PC

"Marc Demetriou brilliantly takes the life lessons supplied by his immigrant grandfather and applies them to the new millennium. This is an essential read for anyone starting out on a new career or otherwise looking to build a successful life." — Neale Godfrey, Chairman & President, Children's Financial Network, Inc., *New York Times* #1 bestselling Author

Acclaim for *Lessons's From My Grandfather*

"Marc has reached into the soul of his past to share with us the wisdom bestowed upon him by his 'Pappous,' (grandfather in Greek). Having also grown up in a Greek family with strong values, I appreciate how Marc translated those tender moments with his grandfather into meaningful expressions and lessons for a better life. From one heart to another, Marc passes on to his readers a powerful pathway to success rooted in deep family values." — **Jim Kirkos, CEO, Meadowlands Regional Chamber**

"*Lessons from My Grandfather* reflects not only on Marc Demetriou's grandfather Charlie, but in many ways it also brings to life a time that too often seems like the distant past: a time when positive and culturally relevant life lessons were passed down from generation to generation. For all those who struggle today with conflicting generational truths, a sense of generational disconnect, and an uncertainty about the rules of human engagement, *Lessons from My Grandfather* offers a guidebook for the future. Whatever your age or your own relationship with your parents and grandparents, you will feel like Charlie should be the spiritual role model for teaching us all how to believe in ourselves and how to nurture relationships with all those around us." — **Jack Myers, media ecologist and author, *The Future of Men: Masculinity in the Twenty-First Century***

"Marc has tapped into the wisdom of the ages and his grandfathers' teachings and has masterfully applied them to modern-day principles of life and business. His lessons will prove valuable for generations to come." — **Nicholas G. Sekas, Esq., Sekas Law Group, LLC**

"*Lessons From My Grandfather* takes the ageless wisdom of an immigrant who came to this country with nothing, and achieved personal and financial fulfillment. Demetriou captures the essence to the secret of success in business and life, while also leaving you feeling inspired and motivated to realize that anything is possible. This book is a manual for life that everyone should read." — **Mike Michalowicz, author of *Profit First***

"*Lessons From My Grandfather is a must read. Marc Demetriou has skillfully woven together his grandfather's inspirational story with timeless nuggets of wisdom which are necessary to live a successful life. This book will motivate and inspire you to not only reach your highest potential but to create your own legacy of wisdom to pass down to the next generation.*" — **James Miller, Executive Producer and Host of the national radio show James Miller | Lifeology**

"When I saw the book for the first time, my thoughts went to my grandfather on my mother's side. 'Pete' left indelible images, sounds, and smells on my life. So, as Marc shared about his grandfather, I could hear the great love he has and thus the book that tells his and Marc's story of love, commitment, and a passion for living life in all areas, with purpose and a love for service to others. And that can bring you the greatest rewards. I highly recommend you get your copy of Lessons from My Grandfather *and listen to our conversation at RichardDugan.com/tmysradioshow.*" — **Richard Dugan, host of KZSB-AM "Tell Me Your Story"**

Contents

Foreword to the 2023 Edition xvii

Preface: Success Is a Choice xxi
    Why I Wrote This Book xxii
    Get Inspired xxiii
    The Success Industry xxiv
    Choosing Your Best Self xxv
    Reject Despair and Darkness xxvi
    Changing the World xxvii
    A Bit about My Past xxviii
    The Key Takeaway xxxii
    My Core Principles xxxii
    Far More Than the Job and the Money xxxiii
    You Never Stop Building xxxiv
    I Believe in You xxxiv

1. Just Charlie, My Mentor 1
    Charlie's Biggest Lesson 2
    Charlie's Early Life 3
    Formative Years 5
    Beckoning Horizons 7
    The Promise of a Life Uncommon 8
    Aiming for America 8
    Taking Flight 11
    Seizing Opportunity 11
    Charlie and Anna 12
    Making His Mark 15
    The West Side Tennis Club 17
    Enjoying Life 18
    Listening and Learning 19
    Life and Love 20
    Charlie's 15 Principles for Success 20

2. Purpose and Passion 33
Where Purpose and Passion Coexist 36
Be Your Heroes 37
Good Old Doctor Seuss 38
Purpose Equals Excellence 39
The Purpose Driven Life 39
Passion Gives Life Its Meaning 41
Find Your Mentors 46
Find Your Purpose and Passion 48
Do What You Love 48

3. Action and Attitude 51
Living with Action 52
Living with Attitude 53
Your Attitude Is Everything 57
Acting Is Difficult 58
Don't Ever Lead with Your Ego 59
Keep Your Eyes Open: Think and Find Every Opportunity 60
It's Much More Than the Job 60
Be Grateful and Live Gratefully 61
Acknowledge That Nothing Is Final 61
The More Joyful, the More Successful 62
Write the Story of Your Life 62
Twenty-Four Hours and Limitless Resources 63
Mixing It Up to Find Joy and Grace 64
Rethinking Action and Attitude 66

4. The Nature of Success 69
Only You Can Guarantee Success 72
Real Life Lessons on What It Takes to Achieve Success 72
The Daily Success Habits of Wealthy People 74
Striving for a Better Life 76
More Authors Weigh In on Success 78
Seven People Who Changed the World 81
Three Final Arrows 95

5. Building Your Foundation: Time and Tenacity 97
Taking Advantage of Time 98
Respect the Work 102
There's No Shame in Punting
and Switching Gears 105
Polishing Your Personal Qualities 106
Assuring the Quality of Your Product or Service 106
Don't Run 107
Standing Out by Going the Extra Mile 108
Learning from Others 108
Finding Your Own Tech Wizard 108
Remember That Communication Is Everything 109
Taking the Necessary Risks 110

6. Building and Managing Your Network 113
Learn From Everyone 114
Build Relationships to Build Your Best Life 114
Mastering the Art of Networking 117
The Rules of Networking 121
Never Stop Building Your Network 123
Telling the World 124
Managing Your Contacts 125
Your Social Media 126
Final Thoughts 127

7. Off and Running 129
How Hard Will You Run? 133
Conjuring Mr. Rogers 134
Whatever You Are, Be a Good One 135
You're Responsible for Your Own Success 135
"Who Am I?" 136
Charlie and His Lessons 137
The Most Important Habit of All 141
Ready, Set...Give Your Best! 142

Index 143

Dedication

I dedicate this book to my Grandfather, Charlie Pistis. He was my mentor, inspiration, and best friend. He always thought of me as the son, he never had and treated me as such. I learned so much from him about life, business and the pursuit of happiness. I wish he were still here to enjoy this book. I know he would have loved it.

I also dedicate this book to my parents John and Fannie Demetriou. I am blessed and grateful to have such loving, supportive and caring parents.

Dedication

Acknowledgements

I spent countless hours over the last few years of my life preparing this book for publication. I didn't HAVE to write this book but I HAD to write this book. I had a burning desire to share my grandfather and all that he taught me with the world. He was such a gift, and others needed to know why. I was blessed to have him in my life until he passed at 97 when I was 37 years old.

This book is now my gift to all who read it. It is unlike any publication of its kind. It hopefully will motivate you, inspire you, drive you, and most importantly, help you to not only succeed in business, but in LIFE. In these pages I share my grandfather's journey to success, and all the principles that he applied to get there. I also share what I have learned along the way as a successful businessman.

I would like to acknowledge and thank my friend and author, Richard Fritkzy, for his hours of guidance and counsel while writing this book. I would also like to thank my editor and publisher, Michael Roney, from Highpoint Executive Publishing. He was an absolute pleasure to work with, and a true expert in his field. He understood my passion and drive in the pages of this book, and edited it with me so patiently and professionally.

Lastly, I would like to thank my brother, Dr. Christopher Demetriou, sister, Andrea Kalliaras, and brother-in-law, Gus Kalliaras, for their love and support—as well as my three beautiful girls, whom I love beyond words: Alexis, Julianna, and Charley.

Foreword to the 2023 Edition

The past few years have been quite an adventure! So much has changed since the last edition of this book was published in 2019. In 2020 and 2021 widespread business shutdowns completely reset economies and work patterns around the world, and Gartner Research reports that organizations now are facing historic challenges: a competitive talent landscape, an exhausted workforce, and pressure to control costs.

Now Zoom meetings are standard and a vast number of people no longer commute to work five days each week. Instead, a sort of hybrid system has developed, with work-at-home the norm for a few days. According to Pew Research Center, about seven in ten workers who say their jobs can mostly be done from home say they are teleworking all or most of the time. A survey by Wainhouse Research found that reported rates of video conferencing have soared, with 68 percent of respondents participating in video meetings more frequently than before the shutdowns of 2020 and 2021.

Collaborative online working has exploded, while social media has become front-and-center marketing for the vast majority of companies and those who work for them.

Artificial intelligence (AI) is also taking a significant role in this new economy, with some companies using it to pre-screen potential interview candidates, while others are using it to monitor and coach employees through certain aspects of their jobs. AI systems such as ChatGPT are on the cusp of causing even more disruption, taking over some writing and marketing tasks (and more?!) even as I discuss them here!

Because of AI and new external economic pressures, some social researchers warn that the least educated, unskilled, and low-skilled workers may be replaced by automation. Vulnerable workers will likely be the hardest-hit group; some of them might have to work multiple jobs (probably freelance jobs) to sustain a living. Additionally, pressed by these new economic realities, companies have turned to "quiet hiring" —stretching and upskilling opportunities for existing employees while meeting evolving organizational needs.

All this means that you'll now need to work harder and more creatively than ever before to have your best chance at succeeding. You will need to broaden your skill set and enhance your life principles to get ahead in today's world.

Pretty daunting? Well, here's the good news: Despite all of these changes, much remains the same for anyone entering and climbing the proverbial ladder in the business world and in life. I'm talking about building valued relationships, taking risks, believing in oneself, building personal resilience and going the extra mile for yourself and others. These principles have *always* been the keys to success in business and in life regardless of the external social and economic landscape. They are timeless—the same success principles that worked for my grandfather, Charlie Pistis, when he came to the United States nearly 100 years ago.

And that's why this updated edition of *Lessons From My Grandfather* is more valuable than ever—updated for the 2020s, but still showcasing my grandfather's timeless principles at its core. I decided to write the first edition years after my grandpa passed away at the age of 97. The light

Foreword to the 2023 Edition

bulb went off and I said to myself, *you know, it's a shame that he's no longer on this Earth because he was such an amazing man, but now it's up to me to share all of his teaching with the world.* And that's when I got to work on the original manuscript.

My grandfather was a success in life because he just had so much to offer: his personality, his mannerisms, his kindness. His empathy, his humility, his hard work, his ethics, his likability. Just everything about him was amazing.

The lessons I learned from my grandfather are universal and more important than ever to people living today and will remain so for decades to come. Actually, Charlie's principles are common threads that are evergreen—they hold up through the years! I'm referring to concepts such as attitude is everything, remain humble always, be thankful for what you have, remembering that one never does it alone, and believing in yourself, to name just a few.

Life is a journey. It's one step at a time. It's being a good person. It's surrounding yourself with positive people, being a giver and even acknowledging others for their good work, friendship, or just pure kindness. Opportunities will come up in life, and when they do you have to be willing to take a chance, but also put in the extreme effort and hard work that is required.

After reading this book, I want you to be able to say to yourself, "I can change myself to be a better person and I can aspire to be a more successful individual in life and/or in business." Success is truly available to everyone, particularly in today's rapidly changing business and social landscape. So, just go after it!

I wrote this book primarily for you—to help you be successful—but also so all parents and grandparents can understand the enormous influence they can have on their children and grandchildren. As I note throughout these pages, *success is a choice*. Every day you make choices on what you're going to do, how you're going to be, and how you're going to react to the situations that present themselves. As you progress further in this brave new world, I hope that you can take from this book my grandfather's mentorship, wisdom, and teachings to live the life you truly desire!

– Marc Demetriou, March 2023
www.grandfatherlessons.com

Preface

Success Is a Choice

> *"Every man is proud of what he does well; and no man is proud of what he does not do well. With the former, his heart is in his work; and he will do twice as much of it with less fatigue. The latter performs a little imperfectly, looks at it in disgust, turns from it, and imagines himself exceedingly tired. The little he has done comes to nothing, for want of finishing."*
>
> —Abraham Lincoln

I have always been an admirer of Abraham Lincoln. He overcame abject poverty, great tragedy, many losses, and a constant battle with depression to become, arguably, the greatest man in American history. What's more, he achieved all of this without ever betraying his honesty, humility, compassion, faithfulness, and purposefulness—qualities that help to define all who are courageous enough to live their very best life.

Our 16th president, the man who saved the Union and freed the slaves, clearly believed in the power of vision and hard work fueled by passion and pride. That was more than 150 years ago, and his words are still spot-on today. Every one of us ought to be, and *can be* great at what we do—if we choose to be.

Success is never an accident. It is a choice, and despite all protests to the contrary, it has always been a choice—*your* choice. Fulfilling a dream or finding your avocation is a choice. Whether or not you get to do what you love to do in life is a choice.

The decision as to whether or not to make that choice is entirely up to you. With great passion, I urge you to make a determination to do just that—to *choose* what will become of your life rather than to accept what life dishes out or randomly tosses your way. I can promise you that if you say yes to success, life will, no matter the circumstances or the obstacles, inevitably embrace and celebrate you.

You are never too young or too old to make your dreams come true…to choose to be what you want to be.

Why I Wrote This Book

I wrote this book because you deserve and are entitled to lead your best life.

I know that opportunity abounds, and that we are capable of creating a more level playing field on which the blessings and bounty of America can better become the province of all.

I am particularly passionate about this subject because of the lessons I learned from my grandfather, who as an immigrant came here with nothing but brains, determination and ambition, and then created success for himself and his family. He is the driving force behind my own success, and the wisdom I can pass on to you as someone who is looking to begin a career, change a career, or enhance your career or business.

Most importantly, I am dedicating this subject to you as someone who has greatness within yourself (whether you know it or not) and who simply wants to reach the highest level of success in business and life that is humanly possible.

Consider this: There is a power behind Ellis Island immigrants like my grandfather. Understanding the challenges they faced and how they dealt with them in order to achieve happiness and success will give you a distinct advantage in the rigorous environment of business and life today.

As a young person in today's world, understanding and learning from my grandfather's experience can be very powerful for you, even as conveyed through my words in this book. Seeing the timeless dynamics of human interaction, purpose, action and attitude through my grandfather's eyes will give you a powerful advantage as you plan your career and strive to move forward.

So, I have a formula for success to offer. I learned that formula at the heels of my grandfather, along with the guidance and driving force from my mother and father. I nurtured and refined it through building my careers and relationships over the years. It has been tested in the prism of tinkering with other theories proffered by hundreds of other authors and life coaches.

Get Inspired

There are thousands of self-help and motivational books out there, and there is no shortage of business coaches, business strategists, and inspirational speakers. All of those other "how to be successful" books are aimed at young professionals or veteran employees in the real-world business spectrum who are simply looking to do better. *This* book offers a very different aspect that makes it very powerful: using the wisdom of a very wise man who "walked the talk" under very challenging conditions, and succeeded in stunning fashion—with financial success, loving friends and family, and overall happiness. That's pretty inspiring.

So, my objective in these pages is to tap into my grandfather's inspirational life and wisdom in order to get you inspired, helping you to achieve what you really want out of life, and what you want your life to become.

And, I have added a very special focus to this work: students and others who have only just begun to engage the "real world." If you are a student and are wondering or wandering, I hope that you may have a little time on your hands to read these pages, get inspired, and think about what you really want your life to become.

A successful life is out there to be embraced, enjoyed, and celebrated by all. And while there are barriers and pitfalls, there are also many ways to either go through them or around them.

The Success Industry

To write, speak, teach, train, or lead on anything that has to do with fostering success has become its own massive multibillion dollar industry. We're not talking cottage industry, but rather big, *big* business.

There are success magazines and academies of success, success audio lessons, webinars, podcasts, workshops and conventions, and thousands of speakers who are making big bucks selling promises. There are what appears to be a zillion-odd books or so out there. There is so much noise being made about success, so many guaranteed formulas and prescriptions, so many secret or profound or golden 5-point, 10-point, 20-point-or-more "can't lose, easy as tying your shoes, tried and true" programs.

In the midst of all this, there are some truly great thinkers, but there are even more charlatans who repackage what the thinkers have already said, and even more who make a fortune talking about their success and urging you to emulate them—as if all you need is to be them, when you're actually *you*.

There is, needless to say, a fundamental problem with that way of thinking.

Yes, there are great thinkers, but there are many more who couldn't find an original thought if they tripped over one.

Unlike them, I will not offer you any golden or secret laundry list of "to-dos," insisting that they will never, ever fail. What you get here are the musings of a decent man who is a very good student and practitioner of principles that made his grandfather and himself successful—albeit in somewhat different ways. What you get here are the ideas and beliefs of someone who had a good family, great mentors, and a rich legacy passed down to him. What you get are the ideas and beliefs of someone who has built a reasonably successful life.

You get a guy who is ranked in the top 1 percent nationally among mortgage producers, as well as a former co-host on a successful weekly radio program, *The Real Estate and Money Show*. You get an expert who increasingly is in demand as a motivational speaker and business strategist at real estate, business, accounting, legal, and finance forums throughout the region. You get someone who was a keynote speaker, along with Tony Robbins, Barbara Corcoran, and many of the nation's best, at the most celebrated mortgage convention in *America: the Mastermind Summit*.

Most importantly, you get a person who is happy to be *who* he is and *where* he is—in touch with the purpose of his life, with a rich and abiding passion for this subject and a mountain of information to share about the same.

Choosing Your Best Self

So choose—decide to make those dreams come true and envision the life that you most want to live.

Henry David Thoreau wrote, "If you have built castles in the air, your work need not be lost; that is where they should be. Now put the foundations under them." What wonderful words! Today we like to say, "See it, believe it, and achieve it."

Whether your lot in life is destined to be good or great, what I trust you will be, at the very least, is your best self–nothing more and nothing less!

It is what life calls upon you to be, begs you to be, and never stops challenging you to be.

When you say "yes" and reach out to become the best that you can be, I can assure you that you will embark on a journey that is destined to result in your living a purposeful and fulfilling life.

Giving up, on the other hand, is the worst crime that you can possibly commit against yourself. *Avocation* is ever so much bigger than *vocation*. The difference between the two is the stark and telling difference between doing *what you love* and what you must, the difference between *choosing* and just accepting.

Reject Despair and Darkness

You may deeply feel that you have been tossed a bad hand preventing you from attaining your dreams, and that you have no options. I reject that, and so should you. To believe that those sorts of things have the right to define you is absurd. Accepting a fate which is less than your dreams is to color yourself in the darkness of a damnable, unforgiving sense of failure.

It doesn't have to be that way. These things have no claim on you. They are not your life. They must not be your life. You must not quit or bail on yourself. If this were to happen, it would be a tragedy.

We all lose big time and in incalculable ways.

I lose, you lose, and so does everyone else in your life. Our cities and communities and society lose. The possible loss of you and your unique talents would affect us all. We are all in this together. As one human family, we are inextricably connected and we have a duty to care for each other and to hold each other up.

The truth is that you and every other human being in our land look out on a boundless universe of infinite possibility. What a wonder each new creation is, and so is our diversity. All of the great theologians and philosophers have long said that this is so. We are—you and I, and all of us—boundless and inexhaustible possibilities and mysteries. We are capable of moving mountains and of building them.

Every one of us is a profound instrument with limitless potential. Share your gifts with others!

Changing the World

You are invited to change the world. Whether that happens in a big or small way doesn't matter. That will play out in time as you make a difference for others—maybe, for many others.

But that big-picture impact stuff is neither here nor there, for you will, without question and at least, change the world for you and those in your life. That alone is more than enough to both command and deserve the very best that you have to give. To the extent that you rise, so too will your parents, siblings, spouse, children, friends, fellow employees, colleagues, vendors or customers rise. You will, as do we all, come to touch many people, and, quite possibly, far more people than you may ever have imagined.

We know that poverty oppresses and limits, and that where you are born and under what circumstances can present both unique and complex sets of challenges. Of course, this matters greatly, and some will have to fight harder to position themselves to live the life they imagine.

There is no shortage of inequities or disparities and there are many different roads that some will have to go down. When metaphorically apologizing to most Americans, President Kennedy once said, "Life is unfair," which we know to be true.

Still, I write in the face of these truths, because there is a door, a path, a way, a place, and certainly opportunity for all, however circuitous the road.

Sure, the roads for each of us may be different, and some are much harder to go down than others, but I can guarantee you that there is a road to your very best successful life. It is one designed for you in the heavens... you alone.

Maybe, just maybe, more is being asked of you because more is expected of you.

So get on the road designed for you and move in the direction of your good and best life. If you choose to live there and fight for it, I'll wager that you will find all the help that you need along the way.

A Bit about My Past

I have always worked hard, did everything that needed to be done, and still more. It started with my paper route when I was 11 years old, which began in the wee hours of the morning before school and lasted throughout the summer. Each day, I set out at 6:00 a.m., and each and every copy of *The Record* was folded perfectly and placed in the spot that the customer preferred. When the weather was bad, it was always put in a clear protective plastic bag, even if it was to be delivered under a roof or placed in a box.

On time, always!

Be perfect and be meticulous—my grandfather Charlie Pistis, my mom, and my dad always told me this. I took this to heart and it has made all the difference in my life. More than anything else, this work ethic of mine has defined me and carried me forward. That ethic is the foundation of my success. My mom always reinforced that I could be anything and do anything I wanted in life, and my dad always reinforced having the highest morals, values, and integrity.

I was a Boy Scout and I loved it. I enjoyed the study and the tasks performed in earning each merit badge. Once again, the opportunity to give my best and to highly achieve stared me in the face. I was constantly challenged, and I thrive on challenges. I wanted to do well, I went after it all, and I discovered that great honor and recognition came along with doing so and achieving the highest rank in scouting—Eagle Scout. My father's support not only helped me achieve this rank, but also allowed my brother to reach it as well.

In my younger years, I played soccer, football, baseball, and basketball, and I wrestled. I was even in karate for a while. I think I tried every sport available, strengthening my appreciation for what it means to be part of a team.

I attended the business school of Rutgers University. Outside of classes, there was no downtime to speak of, as I was always working.

During the summer I worked in construction, air conditioning and heating, and landscaping. During the school year, I waited tables and bartended at a Bennigan's restaurant.

I graduated in 1991 with a high grade point average and a Bachelor of Science in Finance. The time then had come to move beyond the educational and familial cocoons. At this great moment of reckoning, it was time for me to begin proving what I had started believing so long ago about myself.

Prior to graduating, I went to a job fair at Rutgers. There I was engaged and later pursued by a young and hungry firm interested in hiring self-starting mortgage loan officers who could learn on the fly and hit the ground running. From their office in Rutherford, located in Bergen County, which happened to be one the richest and most populated counties in New Jersey, I got busy making money for myself and the company.

I applied my core principle devotion to the job and task at hand. I started early, worked late, spent my lunches doing business, and tried my best to be devoted to our family's "be meticulous and be perfect" mantra.

I first approached every family member and friend, and then I never stopped cold calling. I'd go into any law office, accounting office, real estate office, any and every service or business service organization to make my pitch. I'd speak to anyone there who was willing to give me some of their precious time.

I was first selling myself, and then my company and our ability to both help and serve them in a manner that far exceeded the efforts of any bank. I was on my own and my job was to build relationships and drum up business. It was work that I was born to do.

You had to have the courage and conviction to suffer through nine "no time, no thanks" responses in the hope of winning that one "ok." It would often take more than that 10 tries before I received a "yes." Patience, perseverance, and persistent enthusiasm were key.

Soon I was not just making it, but doing extremely well. Obviously, this kind of work demanded good people skills and what a teacher of mine called "an inherent gift of gab"—all skills that, I assure you, can be developed.

After 12 months, I made a career change. I worked at State Farm for eight years, taking advantage of the training that they offered. In addition, and on my own time, I took 13 courses over a 15-month span of time by studying every night of the week and weekends. This resulted in achieving the professional designations of Chartered Life Underwriter (CLU) and Chartered Financial Consultant (ChFC). I knocked them all down and achieved the kind of status that would help me throughout my life.

I eventually became a partner and chief operating officer of Compensation Solutions—a company that specialized in providing payroll and human resource services and training for corporate clients—while also managing a 401(k), group and individual insurance products, and workers compensation insurance for the company.

Working closely with the president, we built out that company, and it was a great ride, for we indeed succeeded. With more than 500 corporate clients, we managed more than 6,000 worksite employees with what was eventually to become more than 50 in-house employees.

Dealing with both big and small firms, but largely mid-sized companies, we built a very successful enterprise. I had eight successful years there, and we received numerous awards and recognitions. I personally received the "40 under 40" award, which recognizes the 40 most successful businesspeople under the age of 40. As a company, we were also nominated and became finalists several times in the Ernst & Young New Jersey Entrepreneur of the Year Award.

In that eighth year, however, I felt the movement of time's sweet chariot rushing by, as well as the call to build something new, resulting in my good and appreciative partners buying out my interest in Compensation Solutions.

It was then that I met Tom Marinaro of Residential Home Funding, who served on the Meadowlands Regional Chamber of Commerce Board of Directors with me.

I opened my first mortgage branch of Residential Home Funding office in August 2005. I enjoyed 15 years of success there until I was recruited away by Guaranteed Rate in January of 2020. Even at Guaranteed Rate, I continue to be ranked in the top 1 percent of mortgage originators in the United States. I have been listed among the top 100 power players in the mortgage industry, and am among the Top 25 Most Connected Mortgage Professionals in the country.

The Key Takeaway

Here is a key takeaway from all of this: When you do something very well, people stand up and pay attention. That attention will take you places and opportunities open up all over the place. More importantly, people will want to refer business and become a client because they recognize you as an expert in your field.

I co-hosted *The Real Estate and Money Show* on WVNJ radio with one of the top real estate agents in the greater New York and New Jersey area, Antoinette Gangi. It was a great success that helped me become a guest on other shows and accelerated my speaking opportunities.

And things keep getting better! I generated $170 million in new mortgage loans in 2021 and $162 million in 2020. All of the hard work and dedication to be the best that I can be have ultimately led to successful careers and years of enjoyment!

My Core Principles

First and foremost, my core principles were formed by my beloved grandfather, Charlie Pistis, whom you will get to know much better in Chapter 1. He and his life's journey inspired me to reach for the stars, achieve greatness and never give up. He was one of my biggest supporters and looked at me as the son he never had. Consequently, I worked very hard at every job I ever had.

I did so for three very important reasons.

First, to honor and respect the work itself and to bring to it, as one should always do, my very best—even if it was for the sake of the dignity of the work alone. This is a core principle, for no matter the job, it is to be done as well as humanly possible.

Secondly, to impress my superiors with my willingness to go beyond what was required, and to excel—even if it was for the sake of excellence alone. This is a component of the core principle noted above, for to live your best life requires giving your best always. At the risk of being redundant, when it comes to your job, I'll keep reminding you to be meticulous and to strive for perfection, always.

I don't see this as redundancy, but rather emphasis.

And finally, to put myself in position for a raise or for a promotion and prospective advancement—even if these were not possible at the moment. But dedicate your efforts and give your best, and those rewards will most certainly and inevitably come.

Far More Than the Job and the Money

Of course, success is not just about more money. While more is always better than less, success as defined in these pages is so much more:

- It is about family, contentment, and love.
- It is about purpose, meaning, and fulfillment.
- It is about giving back and serving others through charitable causes.
- It is about citizenship—taking part, lending your voice, and doing your duty.
- It is about being the good neighbor and the good person who lives to lend a hand, and who asks, "If it is not about my brothers and sisters, then what and why?"

In other words, success is about the whole package, both the work you do and all of life that surrounds it.

Of course, you can be successful at business and earn more money than you could possibly ever use, ignoring the rest of the world if you so choose. But that could never lead to your best life. To live as such is to live among the lonely and the desperate.

You Never Stop Building

Your success may not be finally manifested in a year, a decade, or even 30 years. As you grow, so too will your success—for once you taste it, you will never stop building upon it.

In doing what you dream and what you love, in blending vocation and avocation, the likelihood is that, even when the twilight bugle summons, there will still be precious pieces of you waiting to be born and realized. You'll still feel, as Robert Frost long ago suggested, that you have "promises to keep, and miles to go before you sleep."

I Believe in You

Let me conclude this preface by loudly saying that I believe in you, and that I have great faith in your hopes and dreams. If you're still among the cynics and the skeptics with regard to your own prospects, I ask you to put the fear and anxiety aside. My job is to change your mind about that, and I intend to do so. We still have time on our side and a book to read. But my first and final objective is to get you to say:

"I BELIEVE IN ME!"

And, even more importantly:

"I WILL SUCCEED AND BE THE VERY BEST THAT I CAN BE!"

1

Just Charlie, My Mentor

"If you are always trying to be normal, you'll never know how amazing you can be."
— Maya Angelou

Our personal stories often reveal what our greatest philosophers and authors cannot. Our stories focus our hearts and souls upon essential truths. That is because our hearts and souls well remember what the mind so easily forgets.

So it is best for us to begin our journey with a great story—the story of a simple and humble man, a poor immigrant who arrived in America and made his way through Ellis Island with nothing but hopes and dreams in his pocket.

No money and no prospects—just a bag full of dreams!

I'm talking about my grandfather, Haralambos Georgiou Pistis—or just "Charlie." He was "Papou" (or "Pappous") to me, which is "grandfather" in Greek.

Heralded in life only by those he served, and by a family that loved him, he would forever remain a simple man. There would be no newspaper headlines touting his accomplishments, no state or municipal proclamations acknowledging his contributions, and certainly nobody bowing in reverence before him.

But what he *did* do, in profound ways, was move heaven and earth for those he loved.

He would literally and forever change the world for his children and his children's children. Through his innate willingness to work hard, and a determination to control life rather than allow it to control him, he went forward through a life that was indeed very uncommon. In doing so, he taught me that succeeding in life was neither mysterious nor complex.

He truly made success simple.

In doing so, he lived large.

As a child, he looked upon America as the "Land of Opportunity." To him, it was *"the light, the lamp, and the golden door,"* and to it he would come.

Charlie's Biggest Lesson

One of the most stark and telling lessons that Charlie taught me about success was that you must treat every single person you deal with as if he or she matters more than anyone else on earth. Be it family, friend, customer, colleague, or client—give that person the very best that you have to give in that moment. That was, to Charlie, the most important key to unlocking the door to success.

When you are good and decent to others, 99 percent of people will, given the opportunity, reciprocate and be good and decent to you in return. When people clearly get your very best, and you demonstrate how much you care about their needs or feelings, they will jump through hoops on your behalf.

It's just the way human beings are wired.

It naturally follows that in giving your best, you will do more than what is required, come in early, work late, skip lunch, go out of your way, put yourself on the line, and make many other sacrifices. Your best is naturally extraordinary, and if you dare to be extraordinary, you simply cannot fail. You will develop equally extraordinary habits, at home and at work, that quite simply assure success.

Everyone my grandfather served in his working life could well have been a king or queen, for he treated each of them with such rich and abiding respect.

Success for him was rooted in the very virtues and qualities that he manifested. These included humility, faith, courage, independence, responsibility, duty, decency, compassion, goodness, and pride. And, just as Robert Fulghum told us some 25 years ago in his powerful essay, *All I Really Need to Know I Learned in Kindergarten*, my grandfather too knew how important it was to "share everything," "play fair," "be aware of wonder," "live a balanced life," and, of course, "not hit people." (The flip side of not hitting, of course, is to support and deliver for them.)

My grandfather, Charlie, knew that he had to "clean up his own messes," "learn some, think some, and work some every day," and "hold hands and stick together."

He knew that he had to set his own table and "put things back where he found them." He knew that the willingness to give all he could to whatever enterprise he engaged would make all the difference in his life. So he would work even harder and give more than others.

His was a humble but profound philosophy that was formed in the crucible of his stoic determination to advance and to succeed in life, despite the challenges and hurdles placed before him.

Charlie's Early Life

My grandfather was christened Haralambos Georgiou Pistis. Many Greeks with the name Haralambos end up being called Charles or

Charlie. So, to those he loved and to those he served, he was and will always be known as Charlie.

He loved to talk, and he took care to speak with me very often. I made it a point to listen, to *really* listen. Eventually, I also made it a point to take notes, because this homespun wisdom just kept flowing out of him, and I wanted to memorialize both the words he spoke and the man himself.

While a project like this book was not even remotely close to my mind at the time, it was good that I kept jotting down his constant musings, because once my lightbulb moment hit, years after his passing, I realized that I had gold to share.

Growing up as he did on a small but beautiful Mediterranean island village, the horizons beckoned brightly from beyond the sea and rough-hewn brick homes. But, as horizons often do, while they beckoned, they did not satisfy. He was only a boy, but even then, he was keenly aware of their presence and how they both teased and invited him. He could take no quantum leaps in his dreams, but he could close his eyes and imagine. What was out there beyond those horizons, he thought?

It is in the nature of horizons to call but not necessarily claim. It is in the nature of horizons to remain elusive to all but the brave. Charlie discovered this in his youth.

He also discovered how critically important it is to "LOOK"—as Fulghum loudly proclaimed in his acclaimed "kindergarten" book—in order to discover the promises that were hidden within those horizons.

I know this because my Grandfather Charlie told me so.

As a small child in the village of Kyrenia on the island of Cyprus, Charlie rode with his father on the front seat of a horse-drawn coach or wagon. There was nothing fancy about it, for his dad's coaches were all buckboard and splinters. He sat on the right, but he was neither a navigator nor a shotgun.

There was no childish fancy about those earliest journeys, for the horse-drawn wagon was the village taxi. Charlie just kept his dad company as people in the village, largely those too old or too feeble to walk, were shuttled from one place to another over rugged cobblestone, hard edged rocks, and ancient earth.

Of course, certain routine tasks, like feeding and brushing down the horses, or cleaning the stable or washing the coaches, were increasingly assigned to him from a very young age. He kept the fledgling family business alive.

By the age of seven he knew that it was his duty to work diligently, for opportunities in his family's small Cyprus village were limited and all businesses and entrepreneurs struggled in the land where he grew up.

Since his eyes, mind, and heart were open, he also noticed and appreciated the stark contrast separating his father's struggle for daily survival, and the dreams out there in those always-beckoning Mediterranean horizons.

In 1916, in the small village of Kyrenia on the island of Cyprus, Charlie's village, life was lived somewhere between the warmth of the sun, the music of the sea, and the simplicity of an unforgiving, yet somehow bearable poverty.

Formative Years

In those earliest of days, Charlie became keenly aware of three thoughts that were to pointedly shape just who and what he was destined to become: the poverty that surrounded him, the lack of opportunity there, and the horizon beyond the sea that beckoned him always. The latter stood out in stark contrast to the former.

The air was filled with the scent of the sea and the olive trees, and of the fresh bread that was baked right within the rock walls of surrounding mountains. The bright rays from the warm sun radiated down from the almost always perfect blue sky. In the Kyrenia of 1920, a village of 2,000, people tilled the land and cast their nets into the depths of the Mediterranean, just as saints and philosophers did some 5,000 years before.

It was the same Mediterranean that Plato and Socrates knew, that Alexander the Great and Julius Caesar knew, that Peter the Fisherman knew, and that Haji Pistis, Charlie's grandmother, knew. His father's mother, she was a respected healer with a mystical aura about her. She was old school, old world, and a link to ancient and noble heritages. And like many religious women, she herself had been baptized in the River Jordan.

Charlie Pistis came from stock that knew something about those keys of the kingdom. His parents were Georgiou and Athena. Simple and hardworking, they taught him all he needed to know about work ethic and the value of treating others with respect and decency, values that would loom large throughout his life.

Charlie vividly recalled that his dad, while pressed by the needs of his own family, religiously helped out others in the village who were struggling. "My dad lived the gospel of Christian charity and he was loved by so many in Kyrenia for what he did. While it always meant less for us, my mom would smile and say 'you know your father.'" Athena, it seems, partnered with him in these manifestations of goodness.

He had an older sister, Katerina, and a brother, John, who was two and a half years younger. Charlie described their family life as normal and happy. "Neither of my parents was ever harsh or mean to us," he said, and he and his siblings always knew that they were loved and valued.

In his nineties, he seemed surprised that his memories of the stable were much clearer to him than those of his home. "I think it's because we spent so much more time in the stable cleaning the coaches and tending to my dad's horses," he said. His recollection was that his dad had as many as 10 horses and no less than three coaches, one or two designed to transport people and the other to transport goods. "One way or the other, however, I recall thinking that my dad was always moving, always in motion," he said.

He took note, even as a child, that one of the secrets in life was to keep moving as his dad had done.

"The great journey of life," Charlie noted, "was this endless array of smaller journeys. It was easy to see this through the work that my dad did."

Beckoning Horizons

As Cypriots, Charlie's family members were then citizens of Britain, part of that once great empire upon which the sun never set. To be a Cypriot, of course, was to be well aware of heritage, for they had rich roots in the epic adventures of the human species, extending back to the dawn of civilization.

Charlie Pistis knew that to be a Cypriot was to be deeply rooted.

He was born in 1909, and the tapestry of his own story would depict one awful war to make the world safe for democracy, the Roaring Twenties, the Great Depression, the evil of Adolf Hitler, the darkness of the Cold War and the Nuclear Age, the great tragedy of 9/11, the onset of a war on terror, the prodigious advance of technology, and ever broader parameters encapsulating the capacity of humanity to both heal and destroy.

Eventually, he became a U.S. citizen, living in New Jersey and Florida, but those frozen images of buckboard coaches in 1916 never left him.

7

In his 90s, he could still hear the rhythmic breathing of tired horses who earned their keep transporting the townsfolk. He could still see the small rise on the crest of the hill by his four-room home, beyond which the sea, the sun, and the always present, always beckoning horizons loomed.

There, the cries of welcome from other children in the village. There, the tanned faces and soft smiles that filled the spaces between the mountains and the shore.

The Promise of a Life Uncommon

There, what was, for him, the promise of a life uncommon, beyond the limitations and poverty of Kyrenia and Cyprus.

A young Charlie Pistis always looked beyond and dared to see what others did not see. He knew early on that there were no limits or ends, so long as one had faith enough to risk, dare, and go boldly into the unknown.

He wondered and imagined what was out there in that horizon for him.

He looked out upon the sea into a vast unknown that beckoned and did not frighten.

He didn't have to read Horatio Alger to know where his dreams lay. He had only to follow the mass of humanity that had already been clearing the path in the great migration to America. That emigrant spirit burned within him, and the light, the lamp, and the golden door led to the answer.

Aiming for America

He had yet to see her, of course, but Lady Liberty in New York Harbor, the one inviting the world to send its "tempest tossed" to her, had begun to take up residence in Charlie's heart.

At the age of 16, it was, for him, time to make his move. It was 1925, and while he was thousands of miles away from the wellsprings of the disaffected, nihilistic angst that flowered in Paris, London and New York City at the time, a different tension and angst burned in him.

For philosopher Jean Paul Satre, America was all about *existential nihilism*—the lack of any worthwhile meaning in life—while writers such as Hemingway and Wolfe focused on discontent and the search for meaning. For Charlie Pistis, America stood for a better life and a purpose that hung out there on the cusp of a vague dream, beyond an ancient and seemingly indifferent sea.

Determined, scared, uncomfortable—yet absolutely certain—Charlie Pistis knew that he must go.

He wanted no farewell and no feelings that might deter him from his course. He wanted to leave without reckoning with the concept of leaving home, for all that he loved there would be carried within, and that which bound him to the heritage that filtered through the air of every soft Kyrenia breeze would forever bind him to those he loved there.

Filled with mixed feelings, he determined to leave Kyrenia and go where one's desire to succeed could be rewarded.

"For as long as I can remember, I longed to get ahead in life," he said. "So, I decided to put the fear of separation from my family aside, to make my plans, and to leave unannounced." To do otherwise, he felt, may well have broken his resolve.

Charlie recalled the emotional start of his journey:

> I remember being down by the docks, waiting to board the ship that would carry me to Athens, Greece, what would be the first stop on a long and uncertain adventure. I managed to work out a deal

with a local merchant to allow me to tend and feed the livestock being shipped to Greece in exchange for a free ride.

A friend and confidante, however, must have alerted my father, so I was surprised to see him approach me. I then was even more surprised to discover that he had come neither to reproach me, nor to condemn my action, but rather to support me. With a weary and resigned look on his face, he simply placed some money into my hands, placed his arm around my shoulders, and wished me well on my journey.

Oh what a bittersweet moment, it was. I can still see the sadness in his eyes, and I could imagine the tears that were to later flow from my mom's eyes when she learned what I had done. Not knowing if I would ever see him or my mother again, it was the kind of moment that lingers in one's soul.

Charlie Pistis was steeled by the dignity and strength of his father, who was willing to let Charlie go. Of course, he needed Charlie's help at home, but there was neither a thought about himself, nor about the assistance that he was losing. In selflessly blessing the flight of his own son, he inadvertently gave Charlie the wings upon which to fly.

"I was never more scared nor lonelier than I was that first night on the ship, but no matter those feelings, I never lost my resolve," Charlie recalled. "I had to grow up fast, and work to make my way, because the little money I had wasn't going to take me very far."

For the record, he did get to see his mother again, as he got to make two trips back to Cyprus in later years, but, sadly, his generous and good father, Georgiou, died painfully of diabetes at the age of forty-nine. While in America, Charlie always sent back money to his parents several times a year. He always wanted to make sure they were taken care of.

Taking Flight

After two years of working an array of jobs in Greece, Charlie continued his adventure to London. Once again, he managed to barter his services as a dishwasher on the transport ship that carried him from Athens to London. There, he found comfort, friendship, and support at a rooming house on 24 Denmark Street in West London, where a number of Cypriot emigrants resided. He also first met Gus Picas, who was a great help to him at the time and who would remain a lifelong friend.

"I discovered that there was never any problem getting work if you were willing to get your hands dirty and put your pride aside," Charlie said. "At the time, I was just struggling to survive and all work had its honor."

Dishwashing led to bussing tables at the Langin Hotel, and later to waiting tables at London's famous Piccadilly Hotel, where he would one day enjoy a reunion with his brother, John. "We were both struggling to make our way, but the common denominator was that we were committed to making our way," he said. "And that is what we had to share with and give to each other, beyond our nostalgic attachment to Kyrenia."

Having finally saved enough, Charlie traveled to the United States on a ship that appropriately bore the name, *The Majestic*.

He did not enjoy the fine dining or the ballrooms on that trip, as he sailed in steerage in the ship's hull with the rest of the "tired, poor and huddled masses" who longed for a better life.

Seizing Opportunity

Charlie came to America in 1929 and saw the Great Depression drive economic opportunity into the ground, and yet the country still held out such promise to him. "When I first saw the Statue of Liberty, she

seemed as big as my dreams and oh what a wonder it was to see her personally welcoming me. I felt honored and blessed. I felt as if I was finally home."

Depression or no depression, he again bonded in a rooming house with friendly Cypriot emigrants, and it took him no time at all to find a job at the Morris Restaurant at Broadway and 46th Street. "Yes, I was doing the grunt work, the menial work, but it was work, real work," Charlie noted. "It was the way forward. It was the beginning."

Putting pride aside, he committed to staying late, working harder, and advancing. The way he saw it, opportunity was opportunity was opportunity. To Charlie, just getting in the door was seizing opportunity.

"That there was always work was such a blessing," he said. "Even in the worst of times like then, there was work for one like me, for one who simply didn't care about diving into the muck."

Charlie and Anna

The theologians and mystics remind us that with God, it is all one. One covenant and one promise! One human family! One binding connection! Such a concept had everything to do with the comings and goings in the life of Charlie Pistis, and his willingness to stand on the edge and leap.

When he left Kyrenia, he also left the young girl who was destined to be his bride.

It would have made great fiction, for Anna was the beautiful young girl he passed by in his father's coach, the one with a most adorable smile, the one he knew would one day be the most beautiful of women. As fate would have it, she was also the daughter of the richest man in Kyrenia.

In Anna, fate, fiction, and reality brushed up against each other. She wasn't even a teenager yet, and she knew nothing of what a young Charlie Pistis saw in her beaming smile or budding beauty. In fact, he used to joke with her that he was going to marry her one day.

But like everything else that was good in Kyrenia, the image of her Madonna-like face also traveled across the oceans with him. It went with him to Athens and to London and to New York City. The smile, the wave, the innocence—a silhouetted vision of young beauty in the Cyprus sun!

After unfortunate and convoluted circumstances, her family traveled to America for a fresh start, and the bright, cheerful, young girl he waved to from his father's coach, the one who smiled back at him always, would come to be his wife.

It was no easy journey for Anna. While in Cyprus, her father was one of the wealthiest people on the island. As a banker, he borrowed money from one man and made loans to individuals and businesses for many years. Unfortunately, the man died and his kids wanted all the money returned, which caused him to liquidate everything to just pay back the loan. He made the decision to leave Cyprus and come to America for its endless opportunities.

Fortune had it that, just as Cypriot immigrants formed a conclave in London, so too did they come together in New York City. In the interest of mutual love and empathy, those who had come earlier were there to support those who had arrived more recently, and Charlie Pistis was there to help the once richest family in Kyrenia find their bearings in America. Social welfare was not yet the province of government, as Franklin Delano Roosevelt's New Deal was only just in a state of becoming.

Indeed, social welfare was the province of one's own people, and Charlie was among the Cypriot brethren who were there for Anna's own. And what was once but a passing fancy was now, in this new world, the stuff of unimagined reality.

Charlie and Anna fell in love. Looking to marry, they had to sidestep convention and cultural protocols which required the older sister to be married first.

"I had to go out and find a husband for her sister, Tessie, first, because she was the oldest and the custom was for her to get married first," Charlie told me. "So I did, great matchmaker that I was."

Charlie and Anna joined hands and lives on August 30, 1936, 11 years after he first left Cyprus. It was a simple ceremony, and he rented the backroom of a local restaurant, where he draped low lying soft lights. With food that family and friends prepared in abundance, along with good wine and a one-man band who could play soft music that touched the heart, they had what Charlie described as a "beautiful reception, one that was worthy of Anna and the beginning of our life together."

So, while the Great Depression was in full flower, FDR's New Deal policies were just beginning to impact America's economy, and Adolf Hitler was flexing the fascist muscles of his Reich, unbridled joy reigned in the world of Charlie Pistis, for the beautiful, young Anna of his dreams had become his.

Charlie had Anna, and he had work to do, along with plenty of happiness and possibilities.

Making His Mark

Over the years, Charlie and Anna would move from Harlem to the West Side, and then to Washington Heights. They spent years at 102nd and Columbus Avenue, and later at 167th Street, raising two daughters, Athena and Fannie. Inevitably, they crossed the Hudson to Bergenfield, New Jersey and ultimately to a second home in Clearwater, Florida, with a last permanent address in Pompton Lakes, New Jersey.

Charlie was proud to have been a Seaman First Class in the United States Navy in World War II, and to have been on a transport ship that was providing support on D Day. He stayed close to those he served with and often spoke of the ironic sadness he felt in transporting German prisoners of war.

"The degrading and inhumane treatment that they received bothered me greatly," he said. "Sure, they were the enemy, but they were just men torn from life like we were. I just thought that we were supposed to be a better and more compassionate people."

It was at the Zeta Psi Fraternity House on 39th Street in Manhattan where Charlie made his first lasting mark in the working world, serving as chief steward to the fraternity brothers. It was a mini-hotel where Zeta Psi members could stay in the Big Apple on a cost-effective basis while exploring any New York opportunity. They also gathered there for meetings and celebrations.

Founded in 1947 at New York University, Zeta Psi is a premier international men's fraternal organization dedicated to forging academic excellence and life-long bonds of brotherhood. Now in 50 major Universities across the United States, Canada, and the United Kingdom, Zeta Psi has produced gifted writers, governors, presidential hopefuls, and the CEOs of major corporations.

Charlie's job as chief steward was to assure that the operation ran smoothly. It was all about clean rooms, fresh linens, good meals, and the unique tastes of the brothers.

Charlie provided to them much more than mere operational efficiency. He gave his heart, soul, and wisdom to them as well. And not only did he come to be treated as one of them, as a brother, but he came to be the one that they sought out for counsel and company. He himself became a destination.

Highly successful college grads, in great numbers, looked to him—the one who had to leave school in what would have been the equivalent of his sophomore year in high school—for counsel.

His Zeta Psi boys came from universities such as Yale, Cornell, Ithaca, Rutgers, NYU, Stanford, and Southern California. They were the publishers and the editors of magazines like *Collier's*, *Parade*, and *McCall's*. They ran steamship lines and printing firms; they were accomplished accountants, lawyers, and investment bankers. They were the entrepreneurs who participated mightily in the drama that reinvented the American economy after the Great Depression and World War II.

Charlie eventually moved on from the Zeta Psi home, but not before they held a banquet in his honor, and officially designated him an honorary fraternity brother, calling him "Mr. Zeta Psi."

The West Side Tennis Club

Charlie's next job was at the club that hosted the U.S. Tennis Open, during his tenure until 1978. The West Side Tennis Club in Forest Hills, Queens was and remains a world-class, private recreational facility with a country club atmosphere in the heart of New York City. Covering 14 acres of open space, it is an oasis of 38 tennis courts of grass, clay, and deco turf.

At the West Side Tennis Club, Charlie brushed up against and befriended many of the truly rich, famous, celebrated and powerful. He served John Fitzgerald Kennedy, his wife, Jacqueline, Frank Sinatra, Johnny Mathis, Perry Como, and Judy Garland. "My job was their happiness," he'd say. "I took care of them and their needs. Judy Garland would present me with bottles of wine and champagne to thank me, and Frank Sinatra, a frequent customer, gave me carte blanche with his account, literally trusting me to take care of his friends in his absence."

He attacked this job with unparalleled zeal.

Long before the Ritz Carltons and the Amazons wrote the book on integrated marketing, and long before they and other great companies began keeping dossiers on the fine details of their customer's tastes, Charlie mastered the art. Focus for him was always on the subtle nuances that made the difference for each customer.

He knew their pet peeves: what kind of towel they preferred, the type of champagne they liked, who wanted well-done and who wanted rare, how much ice they preferred, who liked garlic and who didn't. He was meticulous and attended to the minutest of details.

He was so good at what he did that he was loved by those he served.

Enjoying Life

Charlie would move on from the West Side Tennis Club at Forest Hills to manage the Downtown Angler's Club that was comprised largely of Wall Street investment bankers who looked at themselves as world-class champion fly fishermen. Everything was first class and top-of-the-line when they met at the Fraunces Tavern on 54 Pearl Street, in the very building from which General George Washington said farewell to his officers "with a heart full of love and gratitude."

Fraunces Tavern was where the New York Sons of Liberty met, and where a fledgling national government of the new United States of America, under

the Articles of Confederation, took shape. Many of President George Washington's cabinet officers and their small staffs were housed there.

As an immigrant who found life and fortune in America, Charlie was so proud just to be working in what was to him a hallowed place of honor.

As he had done at the Zeta Psi home and at the West Side Tennis Club, Charlie listened to and learned from everyone around him. He learned about the stock market and investing from some of the best. Everyone you pass on the street has something to teach you, he always said.

"You can learn something from everyone," he would say. "Don't think you know it all. So, don't ever look down on anyone." He served the barons of Wall Street and he took with him the best by way of the knowledge, advice, and friendships that they had to offer.

Listening and Learning

Charlie listened all of the time, and in listening, he learned.

More importantly, he acted upon what he learned. He didn't need a broker or counsel when he began trading stocks and commodities, because he had listened to the brokers and investment bankers at Zeta Psi, to the West Side Tennis Club, and to the movers and shakers at the Wall Street barons at the Angler's Club.

He went to school by educating himself in their company. "I knew that everyone I met had something to teach me," he said. "Being smart is recognizing that everyone you pass in life has something to offer or to give you and that everyone knows more than you do about something."

Charlie made a good living doing his job, but his great success was in applying what he learned by simply listening to and learning from those he worked for.

Life and Love

Charlie would lose his beloved Anna far too soon, but he had his two daughters, Athena and Fannie, his son-in-law John, grandkids, great grandkids, and other family members who were all a very big part of his life until his passing many years later at the age of 97.

Charlie Pistis smiled broadly and laughed often, and he worked very hard in the service of others. He listened far more than most, and learned about businesses that were destined to succeed. He studied investment strategies for stocks and commodities. Then he applied the wisdom and smarts, took calculated risks, accumulated wealth, and achieved tremendous success.

He lived larger than most, as only the heartiest of us do. He loved life and everything it had to offer. He loved being around people and enjoying life with them. What a blessed life he had, and all because he had the courage, determination, drive, and faith to leave the shores of Cyprus as a 16-year-old boy to make a better life for himself. And he did just that!

Charlie's 15 Principles for Success

My grandfather wrote down any formula for success, but he talked a great deal to me about life and about how one ought to live. I extracted these Charlie Pistis principles from all that he taught me. And I am quite confident, grandfather to daughter to grandson, that these same principles came to manifest in my own life, career, and success.

Charlie's voice is humble and straightforward. It is honest and certain and sure. There is no overstatement, no hyperbole, and no nonsense. Each quote is a straight arrow.

I loved his voice, his Cypriot moxie, and these principles of his. I trust that you will as well.

1. ATTITUDE IS EVERYTHING.

Remain positive always. Smile always. Your disposition and the way you carry yourself have everything to do with how you advance in life. Give your very best always.

Charlie said:

> "It's all about attitude. Smile at others, open yourself up to them, and 95 percent of them will eventually bend over backwards to help you. People respond to positive people."

> "If you make people feel more alive, they're going to be on your side."

> "People always helped me. There was George Valentine, the president of a steamship line, and Len Weidman, the editor of *Parade Magazine*, and Arthur Motley, the editor of *Colliers Magazine*, all of Zeta Psi. As they became famous, my Zeta Psi brothers, they were there for me, as were the investment bankers at the Angler's Club on Wall Street. They trusted me, believed in me, and they helped me simply because they liked me so."

> "Give people 100 percent of you."

Synopsis: Charlie believed that how you carry yourself is very important. And he believed that good things come to those who are upbeat and positive—and to those who are open and receptive. Smiling all the time, upbeat and positive all the time, he reaped what he sowed.

2. TAKE THE MIGHTY RISKS.

To live is always an adventure, so take the mighty risks. You must be willing to risk and dare if you are to maximize success. Take your best shot.

Charlie said:

"You know that line, don't you? The one that says a ship is safe in the harbor, but that is not what it is made for."

"Life isn't about sitting on the sidelines."

"You have to go to the cliff's edge and leap if you intend to soar!"

"If you don't take any risks, you'll never go forward."

Synopsis: It was Charlie's opinion that opportunities present themselves to all, but that they are fully maximized only by those who determine to go after them. Reservation, fear, and timidity should have no standing. Among the words he voiced most often, risk may well have been on the very top of the charts. He didn't say "gamble." He said "risk," and there's a major difference between the two. Gambling is the province of chance; risk is the province of wisdom.

3. BE RESILIENT, PERSEVERE, AND NEVER GIVE UP ON YOURSELF.

Every person has the capacity to do great things. It simply takes desire and dedication.

Charlie said:

"I never took no for an answer."

"Be determined and never give up on yourself."

"Just make the decision and do it!"

Synopsis: If you carefully calculate the probabilities, if you know your market, and if you have faith in your analytical skills, then don't stand on the sidelines. Go out and fight for what you deserve. Only those willing to pull the trigger and succeed, actually do. Charlie did and he did so very well. He got the "yes"—the raise, the promotion, the new job, that new business opportunity, the all of it. Fight for your yes.

4. EVERYONE YOU PASS IN LIFE HAS SOMETHING TO TEACH YOU.

Everyone knows more about something than you do. So, listen to everyone. Listen, listen and learn always.

Charlie said:

> "I had no formal education to speak of, but I mixed with the right people and learned from them in the school of life."

> "I became my own broker because those I served taught me everything I needed to know."

> "Be quiet, be still, listen, and you will grow."

> "Smart is realizing that everyone has something to teach you. There isn't a person on the street who doesn't know something that you don't."

Synopsis: He emphasized the word *everyone*. He used the term "anyone on the street," and he referred to both the brilliant and the simple alike, because he was certain that everyone had something to offer him, something to teach him. He believed that the truly smart people were those who recognized how little they actually knew, and that it made sense to pay attention to what others might have to share. Wherever he worked, Charlie fed on the knowledge of those he worked with. He was proud of this and grateful for it.

5. NO ONE EVER DOES IT ALONE.

You must attach yourself to those you can depend upon. You must ally, trust, and build with others. Build a team that you can completely rely upon. Learn from everyone willing to teach you something. Give all you can to them, and they will more than return the favor.

Charlie said:

> "To both earn and honor someone's trust was to have done the very best work I could."

> "It is never just about you. Never!"

> "In whatever you achieve, recognize that others are contributing to your success. So, recognize them and thank them."

> "I grew up with the Zeta Psi family, which helped me as much as people possibly could. Even the ones who became rich and famous didn't forget me."

Synopsis: Principles 4 and 5 are very similar, but the latter emphasizes knowledge and the former emphasizes the value of relationship and team. Here, Charlie sounded very much like a coach, like one bellowing loudly in the locker room that there is "no I in team!" But I don't think he was a coach, nor do I believe that he paid much attention to popular sports. I believe that he was simply a very good player. In Charlie, there was no boast or brag. Instead, he bragged only about the others in his life who took time out to teach him and to contribute to his success.

6. NEVER STOP MOVING IN THE DIRECTION OF YOUR DREAMS.

Accomplishing great things is rarely easy—it requires determination, hard work, and focus. Despite obstacles and occasional setbacks, you must commit to always moving forward toward your goals. If you do that, you will achieve success.

Charlie said:

> "There will be good days and bad days, but the secret is to never, ever stop trying. If you make it, you make it, and if you fail, you pick yourself up and try again."

"I bought and sold and bought and sold and lo and behold, on the thirtieth try, I started to make real money."

Synopsis: No analytical skills whatsoever are required here. Call it what you will— going the distance, seeing things through to the end, never giving up on yourself or your dreams. Don't let a lack of self-confidence or faith in yourself ever stymie or cripple you. Don't quit; give your all each time and every time. Opportunities are everywhere. Charge forward with passion, dedication, and commitment and you can't fail!

7. YOU MUST GO THE EXTRA MILE.
Come early, stay late, skip that lunch, and do more–do the same the next day. Be your best self always.

Charlie said:

"God helps those who help themselves."

"If you are not willing to get your hands dirty and do the menial tasks, how do you expect to succeed? To begin, you must dive into the muck and mire."

"If someone else is working at midnight, you better work until 1:00 a.m."

Synopsis: Charlie almost understated this because it was so obvious to him. To be among the best required giving more than others. If you go the extra mile in all things to do with career, you will always be rewarded. There was a simple equation here: Maximum output is destined to achieve maximum results.

8. REMAIN HUMBLE ALWAYS.
Humility is your friend and ego is not. In humility, reject all prejudices and biases which have no place in business. Treat everyone–absolutely everyone– as you would like to be treated.

Charlie said:

> "I was taught early on that all are equal and I was fortunate to grow up free from prejudices."

> "Those who like to boast and brag inevitably lose. You brag and you get nowhere."

> "If you lead with your ego, people don't tell you a thing that matters. They'll keep their distance."

Synopsis: I hear him even now. "You boast and no one will open up to you." Charlie couldn't have been clearer about keeping one's ego in check and giving all honor and glory to either others or to God. He never got lost in his achievement or in his success, and that was truly one of his greatest accomplishments. He knew how to separate "the wheat from the chaff."

9. LOOK FOR WHAT OTHERS DON'T SEE.

Look beyond—look harder and deeper. If you do not look for what is new in each day, so much will pass you by. Opportunities rise up with the dawn just as the sun does.

Charlie said:

> "Every morning is new. Be new yourself."

> "Focus upon your dreams and see what others do not see."

> "Sailing across the ocean was to see and believe in something greater, and so too was putting hard-earned dollars into stocks that weren't that popular. I had to both look into and look ahead and then have faith in what I saw."

Synopsis: You just have to love Charlie, for all of his principles are rooted in this unbridled and simple yet profound faith. He's almost biblical in his wisdom. Eyes wide open, look hard and then move, act, do, and succeed—that is his formula. But it worked only because he bridged the gap between sight and reality and wisdom.

10. BE AWAKE AND ALIVE TO THE SUFFERING OF OTHERS.
Do not pass by their suffering. If you do not live charitably, you will never be whole. Happiness depends on this.

Charlie said:

> "You must give in order to truly live. You must give in order to receive."

> "If you don't give back to your own family and to those around you in need, you are no success."

> "If you don't care, you might have the money, but you will not know happiness."

Synopsis: This is said in The Lord's Prayer and in Saint Francis' Prayer of Peace, as well as in the Koran and the Old and New Testaments—and it was a key tenet of the theology of Charlie's church. But what matters is not that he acknowledged this, but rather that he actively lived it. "I sent money home to Cyprus," he said. "I helped family members who were hurting. I cared for my brother and immigrants. Community was more than a word to me." Charlie gave living expression to what mattered most, so as not to be among the rich who would come to find their passage into heaven to be as difficult as that of a camel trying to make its way through the proverbial eye of the needle.

11. TO WORK IS TO SURVIVE AND THAT IS NOT ENOUGH.
If you want success and comfort or the extras in life, you must do more than work, and more than the ordinary. Extraordinary is about going beyond.

Charlie said:

>"You survive by working. You do more than survive by acting smartly and applying wisdom."

>"It's not your wages that give you a good life. It is your wisdom."

>"I always had money, but only because I used my head."

Synopsis: What you do to live or to exist is one thing, but what you do to excel or garner the edge in life is quite another. So invest, start a business, partner, build upon an idea, create, and reach beyond to garner more than what it takes to merely pay the bills.

12. BE THANKFUL FOR WHAT YOU HAVE.

Whoever God may be to you, be thankful to Him or Her. If you do not believe, be mindful that it is not all about you, and take note of the wonder and gifts that surround you. Humility, goodness, character, and faith are among the mighty byproducts of success.

Charlie said:

>"Goodness prevails."

>"I was a good people person and that's the key. I made it a point always to make people feel at home with me. And it didn't matter to me if they ran a company or held a tin cup on the corner of the street. The least among you deserves even more of you."

>"I thanked God every day for I have been very blessed by Him."

Synopsis: Charlie absolutely associated goodness, character, spirit, and even faith with success. Upon reflection, it became clear to me that he believed that if God was with him, no one could stand against him. Charlie valued decency, kindness, and honor, and he was rewarded for it. No matter how busy, he always went to church. Charlie would often say that he had an angel watching over him, and he really believed it.

13. THERE ARE NO LIMITS AND NO ENDS.
There are only new beginnings. There are and never have been any final victories. The journey always goes on.

Charlie said:

> "Limits are artificial creations."

> "I learned this from my dad: The secret to living is to keep on moving. Action is always the antidote to despair."

> "If you stop going forward, you've quit."

Synopsis: Recently, I read that "every wall is a door." There is, philosophically and practically speaking, always something more, always new paths, new ways, and new opportunities. Charlie consciously attacked each new day with that mindset. Boundaries and limits and ends were simply not real to him. They were but "artificial creations." What power and strength there was in that attitude and mindset.

14. BELIEVE IN YOURSELF ALWAYS.
Believe that you will get ahead, grow, and win.

Charlie said:

> "Life is an odyssey—as a son of Greece and Cyprus, I was one part Achilles and one part Ulysses."

> "I believed that nothing could ever stop me. I really did."

> "It's your world, so damn well act like it."

Synopsis: If you don't believe in you, the likelihood is that no one else will. So believe! No loss should ever deter you from going forward. Remember, believing in yourself is not about ego. It is rather the very fulcrum upon which everything else depends. It is human to doubt and fear, but don't ever let the likes of these take control. You are the master of your destiny. You are the captain of your life's ship.

15. BE JOYFUL.
Find the joy in what you do and prosper. Should you find happiness in what you do, as you should, you will succeed all the more. So look to mesh vocation and avocation, and know that there will be joy enough in the mere pursuit of the same.

Charlie said:

> "For God's sake, I celebrated life when I was a dishwasher. All work has its dignity and honor, but if you sour on the work, still find the happiness in those you work with."

> "When you smile, the whole world smiles with you."

> "I never met a man I didn't like, and I enjoyed every job I ever had. People laugh at me when I say this, but it's the God's honest truth. You see, I just decided to. I made it my habit to. My positive attitude was a relentless force for good for me."

Synopsis: If there was not joy and happiness, I believe that Charlie might have wondered: "Then what, then why?" At ninety seven, he was still such a joyful man. His thoughts and expressions remained so alive and vibrant. He was happiness on parade. There was still joy in his heritage, in his Anna, in his family, and in the "land of the free and the home of the brave." And in me. His positive attitude made it impossible for him to extract anything but joy.

Emulate him and his attitude. Be positive always. Smile. Find your joy and you'll find your success.

Make no mistake about it, Charlie had the talent, the gift, the goodness, the wisdom, the attitude, and the heart that made him, as Robert Burns said, "Is king o' men for a' that."

And while he did not speak to this, it is so important to me. For I believe that there was such energy and power in the can-do, "damn the torpedoes and full speed ahead" immigrant spirit to which he gave such mighty expression. Immigrants came with nothing in their pockets but dreams, and they were not afraid. America was opportunity personified, and it was more than enough for them.

In this, there is much with which we today need to recapture and reconnect.

The next chapter picks up from here and looks at the life I have lived. You'll get to judge just how well I did following in my grandfather's footsteps, and what I did to both refine and build upon his 15 prodigious principles. We'll begin to focus upon my principles and the habits that I religiously employ.

Just like him, I have had a love affair with life, I'm excited for each new day, and I feel blessed and determined to do even more for my family, my many business associates, you, and those who suffer in our midst.

Know that I also am excited to have you on this adventure or journey with me.

2

Purpose and Passion

"You don't choose your passions. Your passions choose you."
— Jeff Bezos

"Take the mighty risks."
— Charlie

Think hard about the clear and compelling quote from Jeff Bezos, founder and CEO of Amazon.com, that appears above. I tend to agree with it, but finding your passions doesn't always come easily. You still have to go deep inside to make a connection with your deepest motivations. Once you do that, you will have the capability to take a provocative journey—one in which you can tap into the power of your motivations to both determine and drive your purpose.

This chapter dwells upon these two strong and formative words—*purpose* and *passion*—and how they can be activated through my grandfather Charlie's core principles. Stop and consider these words. They must be embraced and literally internalized by all who intend to live their best lives. They must become one with your mind and spirit, and imbued into the very fabric of your life.

They are, I believe, two of the most powerful and wonderful words in the English tongue—*purpose* and *passion*. At the epicenter of anyone's best life, purpose and passion are on center stage, living large.

These concepts are replete with strategies that must become habits, the very rules by which you live or by which you govern yourself.

In short, you have got to want it and you have got to want it bad. As you already know, you must be willing to work for it.

The greatest of philosophers, from Socrates, Plato, and Aristotle onward, have long insisted that nothing of true value in this life is ever easily or lightly attained. You have got to want it, and you have to be willing to work hard for it.

ASK THE RIGHT QUESTIONS
Parade magazine and Yahoo! Finance surveyed over 26,000 Americans and found that nearly 60 percent of them regretted their career choices. This is a tragedy of monumental proportions.

Beyond these, many others suggested that they were not entirely satisfied or fulfilled. This means that less than one out of five Americans are satisfied.

In his book, *Springboard: Launching Your Personal Search for Success*, acclaimed Wharton Business School Professor Richard Shell called that result "an incredibly sad statistic," and noted that it was especially so since job satisfaction has become the most critical factor to a person's sense of well-being and overall happiness with life. "So how is it that so many people have found themselves in careers that leave them feeling empty and unfulfilled?" asked Shell. He states that one likely reason is that they didn't ask the right questions at the start.

What a profoundly important observation—*they didn't ask the right questions at the start*. It seems, therefore, that it all has to begin with introspection, with soul searching, with trying to understand just who and what you are.

As Henry David Thoreau proclaimed in his *Walden; or, Life in the Woods*, you must "be a Columbus to the hidden worlds within you." That is, my friends, the most important of all possible explorations, and it's exactly where your journey must begin.

Likewise, as Shakespeare's Polonius cries out, "This above all: To thine own self be true, and it must follow, as the night the day, thou canst not then be false to any man." The very first commitment that you must make is that you will not be among the four out of every five Americans who sadly were not true to themselves.

WHO AM I?

Say it out loud: "Who am I?"

This is the first question, the first exploration, the foundational premise of all that you will do in order to both discover and live your best life. This is the key to your kingdom!

Shell also wrote, "I think that for a lot of these people, they hadn't thoughtfully defined what success would look like in their own terms before pursuing work that aligned more closely with family, social, or cultural expectations. They hadn't thought at the beginning to look for a suit of clothes that would fit them."

We don't, he suggests, look for the suit of clothes that will fit us at the outset. We don't pause, at the outset, to think about the story that we would like to write or live. We don't attempt to define ourselves or how we would like to be remembered.

He goes on suggesting that we must ask, "What makes my heart sing?" or, "What is success for me?" I hear the great character, Bill Parris (Anthony Hopkins) in the movie *Meet Joe Black*, when he was advising his daughter about love and marriage—that she should be deliriously happy, sing with rapture, stay open and wait for "lightning to strike."

It's all too easy for people to still take the safe career path. Shell asks us to be far braver and more daring with our choices and he invokes Steve Job's poignant observation: "Your time is limited, so don't waste it living someone else's life." He passionately asks people to have the courage to follow their own heart and intuition, to follow a path that points them in the direction of what they'd truly like to become.

In other words, live your own dreams. Find your purpose, find your passion—this is exactly where you must begin. Ask yourself, again and again and as often as it takes, "Who am I, anyway?"

Where Purpose and Passion Coexist

So, what will lead you to become self-actualized? Abraham Maslow, the great motivational theorist, defined that as the highest-order motivator, where your purpose and passion coexist. This is where every aspect of your life falls into sync, and where life's most elusive value—peace—lives.

There are, of course, lower-order everyday needs—food and a place to live, for example—which move all of us to act, work, and produce. But the highest-order motivator is self-actualization, where you embrace your destiny, your soul sings, and you are happy.

That's where you are at your best, that's where you make the world better, and that's where you and your very life become an inspiration. It is a place where you are firing on all cylinders, in harmony with your soul and with the universe.

You may well have to start with less inspiring jobs, even menial and unfulfilling work, but nevertheless, you must chart a course and set sail in the direction of your dreams.

What Would Charlie Say?

My grandfather believed in taking risks, and he demonstrated his commitment to that approach throughout his life. He believed that reservation, fear, and timidity should not stand in the way of seizing opportunity, as he did by sailing to America and doing every job he could with unparalleled attention to detail and a maximum commitment to serve. "Life isn't about sitting on the sidelines," he told me. "If you don't take any risks, you'll never go forward."

Be Your Heroes

Wintley Phipps, an African-American entrepreneur, pastor, and singer with a powerful voice, may be one of the most-watched inspirational speakers in the world. He specializes in messages of hope, faith, and imagining the possibilities.

Phipps powerfully insists that you must identify the heroes in your life—your spiritual mentors. It is then incumbent upon you to carry both them and the particulars of their way of being with you always. The heroes Phipps carries with him are a diverse and eclectic group that includes Winston Churchill, George Washington Carver, Martin Luther King, and Luther Vandross.

In one speech, he noted that he was traveling and had the opportunity to visit Winston Churchill's grave on the 50th anniversary of VE Day in 1995. There, he was amazed to see floral tributes from Greece, France, Norway, Belgium, the United States, and elsewhere.

"Amazing, amazing, to see such tributes," he said, "for here was one man, just one man, who saved the world from great evil. One man, who our President Kennedy said, 'commissioned the English language and sent it off to war.'"

Phipps noted that he strives in all that he does to hold on to Churchill's courage. He also carries Carver's relationship with his God and his incessant pondering of the mysteries of the universe, King's passion for justice and dying for what he believed in, and Vandross' ability to paint one thousand colors in a single song.

Good Old Doctor Seuss

The renowned children's book author Dr. Seuss believed in the power that you possess to realize your dreams. While the choices are endless, here are just a few quotes from a vast flowering field of marvelous "Seussisms" that describe being free from the baggage and encumbrances of life that unfairly and unnecessarily weigh you down. Be like the child you once were, who was entirely free to imagine and to dream anew.

- *"Today, you are you, that is truer than true. There is no one alive who is you-er than you."*
- *"You're on your own and you know what you know. And you are the one who'll decide where to go."*
- *"With your head full of brains and your shoes full of feet, you're too smart to go down any not so good street."*

I urge you to listen to Dr. Seuss's words as if you were young (which you well may be), innocent, and free to dream (as I expect you are). Recognize that anything standing between the very real child that you were and you today is just a load of crap. If the story that has been written about you thus far is not what you want, you can simply throw it out with yesterday's garbage.

It's time to write your new story—one that invites you to dream again as a child, explore, and then activate both the purpose and passion within you that will carry you home.

Purpose Equals Excellence

Purpose is that which you were destined to be, do, or become. Your immediate objective is, like Charlie's was, to impress your superiors with your willingness to go beyond what was required in order to excel—even if it is for the sake of excellence alone. To live your best life requires giving your best always. At the risk of being redundant, when it comes to your job, I'll keep reminding you to be meticulous and to strive for perfection always.

Your purpose, in short, is huge in the scheme of your life. It is, at once, your very life's calling, your dream, a primary reason for your being, and the regular and ongoing fulfillment of tasks and objectives, enabling you to deliver your life's goods. Wow!

Purpose is power. It frees people to fulfill their destinies and to remake the world. At its core, your purpose is the very reason for which you exist. It is the intended or desired result of the objectives and the definitive outcome of your life.

Such a simple word, and yet so much is at stake with it.

It is the most basic, demanding, and uncompromising question that you confront in life. Why am I here? What is expected of me? What road, what path, what sail and why? *What is my purpose?*

The Purpose Driven Life

I struggle with the fact that the masses are poor and the few are rich. I struggle with the mere idea that so many people are condemned to poverty, degradation, and oppression, while others have palaces and yachts.

Yet, we are given all that we need—the free will and wisdom with which to make decisions and choices. We get the tools for living. The choices and roads selected, and the ships upon which we sail, are ours to determine.

President John Fitzgerald Kennedy once told us that on this earth, "God's work must truly be our own." That, too, is the work of determining your path and your purpose. The admittedly daunting and necessary task of doing so, therefore, is all yours. It will be you, and only you, with the possible help and guidance of those you trust, who must both *decide* and *do*.

"Woe unto those who get it wrong," you might be thinking, or worse yet, "woe unto me if I get it wrong." So, if you're muttering "holy cow" to yourself right now, believe me, I understand. In fact, to scare you even further, I can reach into my bag of tricks and pluck out the words of Douglas Coupland in his *What Is to Become of Us*, where he wrote: "You keep waiting for the moral of your life to become obvious, but it never does. Work, work, work: No moral. No plot. No eureka! Just production schedules and days! You might as well be living inside a photocopier."

Too bad for him, and for his having to live inside a photocopier, which conjures up far too many strange images. He is welcome to live in his photocopier if he so chooses, while you, most assuredly, need not do so. It is your choice. It is your decision and your determination.

Still, you may wonder how you might "get it wrong."

So what? In golf, we get mulligans, and in life we get do-overs. There are, after all, second and third and tenth chances.

Sometimes, who and what you are, and what you can be, just stare you in the face, and yet you do not see, because the damn trappings of your life engulf you. On a daily basis, you must shake off all that preoccupies and worries you, and just be the child again who innocently looks out into a vast universe and considers that which ultimately matters. Allow your truth to slap you in the face. Allow determined and concerted introspection to give you clarity and answers.

Believe it or not, the answer is always there.

Think of what you have always liked. Take a journey back in time, and consider the toys, the games, the subjects, the books, the shows, the movies, and the people that you most liked and why. What inspired? What moved you? Consider what it was about each one of those things, and start by exploring the common denominators. To whom and to what have you always been drawn?

And bang, it hits you right over the head. You're looking for your "what," only to be struck by the fact that you can't get there without your "why."

Enter passion.

Passion Gives Life Its Meaning

Passion is what you love, what you most enjoy doing, what gets your juices flowing, your heart pounding, and your spirit soaring.

And so, purpose and passion join together in lockstep, forever comingled.

You are struck by the age-old cry of "do what you love, and love what you do."

Interestingly, the word "passion" finds its source in the Latin word, *patere*, which is to suffer. Passion finds its very root in suffering, and in loving so deeply that it hurts. Christians consider the passion of Christ, and the word has long been associated with sex and lust. And yet, for our purposes, it has to do with that force and burning fire inside you that compels you to embrace a field of endeavor or initiative, and to make some kind of difference for the good. Whether for one or two or for many, it does not matter. What matters is only that the ends complete you.

Purpose is the end, while passion is the driver.

What was the common denominator that tied the toys to the subjects in the classroom, to the places you like to go, to the people and the movies that you've loved? Are you drawn to the outdoors or to saving the environment? How about the cosmos or history, or perhaps marketing, retail, or finance? Does public service, education, or diplomacy get you excited? Are you passionate about justice, art, or broadcasting—or perhaps, telling stories, or telling someone how to invest?

The boxes that you might want to click on are literally limitless.

The trick is to find the one where you would like to write the story of your life, the one where you would like to make that contribution to be remembered for.

"The purpose of life," wrote Emerson, "is not to be happy. It is to be useful, to be honorable, to be compassionate, to have it make some difference that you have lived and lived well." It is to find meaning and satisfaction and high achievement and honor, which renders the happiness but a byproduct—a nice one to be sure, but a byproduct just the same.

Together, purpose and passion, the "what" and the "why" of your life, the vocation and the avocation, give you reason to want to get out of the bed every morning. They also give you cause to be excited by what you do, and to find joy in your efforts. Together, purpose and passion conspire to fashion people who succeed both in business and life.

Those who lead their very best lives align what they do or their purpose with why they do it or that which is their passion.

For some, Maslow would tell us, purpose is merely putting food on the table, a roof overhead, and shoes underfoot. For others, it's just being good at what they do—whether it's being a good teacher, a good broker, a good coach, or a good big brother. For still others, it's *striving* to be their best, and for still others, it's the pursuit of happiness. For me, it has become the pursuit of perfection in all aspects of my life, as inspired by my grandfather. Of course, I know that nobody is perfect, least of all me. But in the striving, new vistas and opportunities open up. They just do.

So, in no particular order, I strive to be the best mortgage guy, the best companion, the best father, the best son, the best brother, the best friend, and the best person that I can possibly be. At work, my purpose is to be so sure of satisfying my clients that I can be certain that they'll refer me to their friends and family. As efficiently and effectively as possible, and under the best possible financial terms, my purpose is to help people get into their new homes, or to assist with a refinance to improve their current financial situation.

I also strive to be diligently cognizant of the needs and hopes of all those with whom I do business or associate, and I strive to refer both business and opportunity to them. If you ever allow selfishness in and make it just about you, I can promise you that you'll be traveling, at warp speed, into an empty hole.

It has never been my intention to just get by. Like Charlie, I want to *wow* people with my passion and fervor, and with my attention to every detail. My purpose is to blow people away and exceed their expectations. I strive to be the most dedicated and committed mortgage financier on the face of the earth. I grab the shovel and I start digging. I don't stop until I come up with something that works for each and every client.

My passion takes on its own aura and becomes the magnet that attracts both people and success. It's there in the enthusiasm that I have for my work and in the joy that I find in it. I walk into a networking event, a business luncheon, or a meeting and I get excited to be there, because

I know that I can put my passion on ready display and get those surrounding me to trust me, simply because they can. Of course, I want them to do business with me, but it's also about their allowing me to get to know them and to help them with their work. I love it when a friend introduces me to someone and says, "This is Marc. If you or someone you know needs a mortgage, he's the guy."

I celebrate being "the guy," and am so thankful to be "the guy"—and yes, I am passionate and on fire for it all.

You see, I don't punch a clock, nor do I count the minutes or the hours, because I love what I'm doing. When work is not work to you (and mine is truly something I celebrate), you know you are living in that place where purpose and passion have forged a binding and lasting relationship. I am fortunate enough to be fulfilling my purpose. The passion and love for what I do literally drips from my sleeves, and people can just tell that I'm for real, while they can tell a phony or a pretender from a mile away.

In *Life, Truth, and Being Free*, Steve Maraboli wrote, "You were put on this earth to achieve your greatest self, to live out your purpose, and to do it courageously." Dostoyevsky earlier wrote in his classic, *The Brothers Karamazov*, "The mystery of human existence lies not in just staying alive, but in finding something to live for." It's interesting that both authors, in very different types of books, at very different moments in history, agreed and spoke to the issue of finding purpose and living a fulfilled life.

Live your best life, be purpose driven, be ethical and high-minded, love, and give a damn about the lives of others. Above all, live your avocation and not just a vocation. Be one of those who dares to experience the rarified joy of loving what they do in life. That is the first definition of success. The practical necessities, the money, the security, and all of the rest is secondary.

Purpose and Passion

One of my favorite poems by the great Robert Frost was written about this very subject, the importance of meshing avocation with vocation. Wrapped around a simple story of men who chopped wood, this was the concluding stanza:

But yield who will to their separation,
My object in living is to unite
My avocation and my vocation
As my two eyes make one in sight.
Only where love and need are one,
And the work is play for mortal stakes,
Is the deed ever really done
For heaven and the future's sakes.

Life, he suggested, is meant to be lived where vocation and avocation find each other and where they conspire together so marvelously that "work becomes play." And may I suggest that only in those cases where one lives a best and fulfilled life "is the deed ever really done for heaven's sake."

The path for you is clear, find your purpose and your passion and courageously live your best life and nobody else's. Do the work, chart your course, and set your life's sail in the direction of the dreams that purpose and passion dictate for you.

Do not hesitate, do not pass go. Just start living your life.

Damn the torpedoes that come your way and go full speed ahead. Have faith. Have courage. Trust yourself and keep the words of Dr. Seuss close to the vest. Remember that only "you are you-er than you." No limits, no bars, it's only a mountain that has been placed in your path! All you need do is to pick up the shovel and start digging (or doing the hard work) and you are on your way home.

It is up to you to realize both your purpose and your passion and to become intimate with the life force and fields of endeavor that matter the most to you. It is up to you to seek out the people who can help you, and it is up to you to design a plan and chart a course. It is up to you to make the decisions and to act on them, with boldness, resolve, and dedication. Only you can be fierce for you. It is up to you to adopt and embrace a whole new approach to life, wherein you determine to make what you do and how you live each and every day a masterpiece, better and better and better still as each day passes by.

Find Your Mentors

In this chapter, you already heard from Wintley Phipps regarding the importance of identifying your spiritual mentors. His were as diverse as Winston Churchill and Luther Vandross. I know a guy who has an intimate relationship with Abraham Lincoln, who reads every word ever penned about him, and who is truly inspired by how he lived his daily life. I know others who look to everyone from Bill Gates to Steve Jobs to Robert F. Kennedy to Ronald Reagan to James Taylor to find a singular purpose. Even words and music inspire people to be good, stronger, and purpose driven. I'm confident that you have those who inspire you as well, and I ask you to think about just what it is that you see in or take from them. As you do so, you are nurturing your passion and positively impacting your driving impulses.

Of far greater importance, however, are those in your real or everyday world, who you can access regularly and look to for guidance, support, and wisdom. A mentor is one who is willing to take interest in you and work with you, just like a coach or trainer does. A mentor can help you achieve your objectives, one step at a time.

It could be anyone—a member of your family, a friend, a teacher or professor at school, a counselor at a Boys or Girls Club, or one who has already achieved success or recognition in the enterprise or world that you have set your sights upon. You should know that many organizations and public agencies have formed mentoring circles for those out there seeking direction and guidance. There are also highly successful achievers who take great interest in those striving to make their way up. Seek them out. Do not be afraid to ask. Write those who you would like to reach, and respectfully ask if they would be kind enough to see you. If you need help with formatting the letter, get it at a local school, club, or service organization. In the asking, be professional and put your best foot forward.

Find the best people in your industry or field of endeavor, and ask them if they can help you, or at least if they would be kind enough to point you in the direction of another who might well be more open and willing.

The point is that if you are going in a certain and sure direction, don't ever be afraid to ask for help from those who might help you get there. You may suffer the slings and arrows of a coldhearted few along the way, but, in the end, you'll find your mentors.

As for me, you already know that I was uniquely blessed in that I had parents and one very special grandfather on hand who mentored me from the get-go. They helped me develop habits as a boy that I kept and enhanced throughout my life. Together, they taught me how to develop the tools and the habits that helped to make me an excellent person who was always willing to go that "extra mile."

Let me assure you that finding a mentor is critical—to you, your career, and your best life. Know that they are all around you, waiting and ready to help one like you, who is committed to giving your all, maximize your potential to achieve success.

Of course, they cannot solve every problem or challenge. They must be free to criticize, to cajole, to prod, and to ask more of you. You must be prepared to listen and do your part to earn their continued investment, trust, and faith.

A mentor relationship is about give and take. Yes, it is constructed to enable you to gain, but you also should strive to be helpful in return. Be grateful, share your triumphs and victories, and be open to doing whatever you can to help and serve your mentor in return.

In living and in advancing in the direction of your dreams, there are no, nor should there be, one-way streets.

Find Your Purpose and Passion

I wrote earlier that purpose and passion are as big as it gets and they are. That isn't to say that finding your purpose and passion will be easy. There will be setbacks on your road to success. Remember that there are always second chances and opportunities to recalibrate and adjust. I urge you not to lightly abandon any dream, and to hold fast and sure to that which is right for you.

Do What You Love

Finding and living purpose and passion are indeed the noblest of goals.

There are "Man on Purpose" seven-week adventure courses and "Purpose Prizes." As for passion, there is no shortage of portals, paths, and discoveries. There are books on channeling your new energy, discovering your harmony, self-acceptance, boundless possibility, and soul signatures. The Integro Leadership Institute even fashions "Passion Pyramids" to be pondered.

Passion is a word that inspires thousands of wisdom-laden quotes. I'll close this chapter with a handful of my favorites.

"Allow your passion to become your purpose, and it will one day be your profession."—Gabrielle Bernstein

"Life is nothing without passion."—Emma Michelle

Nelson Mandela said, "There is no passion to be found in settling for a life that is less than the one that you are capable of living."

Simon Sinek said, "People don't buy what you do, they buy why you do it."

Bill Butler said, "Passion is the oxygen of the soul."

And Steve Jobs said, "The only way to do great work is to love what you do. If you haven't found it yet, keep looking. Don't settle. As with all matters of the heart, you'll know it when you find it."

What Would Charlie Say?

Charlie believed that good things come to those who are upbeat and positive—to people who are open and receptive. Success, to him, was also about how you carry yourself, no matter what job or task you are addressing. It's Rule #1: Remain positive always. Smile always. Your disposition and the way you carry yourself have everything to do with how you advance in life. Give your very best always. That is Charlie's example of purpose and passion.

In the following chapters, you'll explore techniques to help you do just that—reach inside to pinpoint your purpose and your passion. Out of that comes enthusiasm, dedication, determination, and excellence—the pursuit of perfection itself, and all of the stuff that actually matters in a life.

Do what you love and love what you do. Don't ever settle for anything less.

3

Action and Attitude

*"Life is like riding a bicycle. To keep your balance,
you must keep moving."*
— Albert Einstein

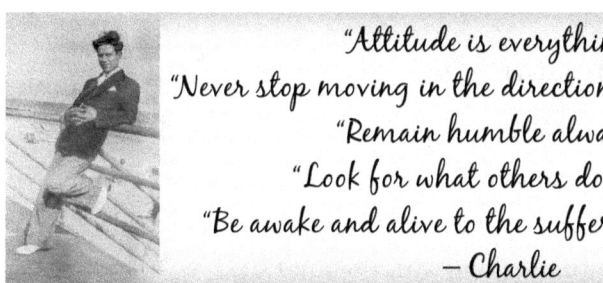

"Attitude is everything."
"Never stop moving in the direction of your dreams."
"Remain humble always."
"Look for what others don't see."
"Be awake and alive to the suffering of others."
— Charlie

In this chapter, I want you to think about two words in a new and different light—two words that literally have everything to do with your life as you go forward to live your dream and fashion your success.

The words are *action* and *attitude*.

How you act, and how you feel, from the moment you arise in the morning to the moment you drop into bed at night, determine whether or not you'll ever live your passion or fulfill your purpose.

These are words with which you must become intimate. Charlie taught me that the journey you intend to embark upon demands that you never stop measuring, evaluating, and tweaking your actions. You also must work to maintain a balanced and constructive attitude—one that you'll be willing to sharply check at the door when necessary.

These are powerful words that have everything to do with success and living your best life. These are words that should speak to you loudly and constantly. They should rise up and come alive in you every morning when you first drop your feet to the floor by the side of the bed.

Each day is ultimately about two things and two things only: what you do (action), and how you react to the same (attitude).

Living with Action

In order to achieve anything, you must be up and doing, actively engaged, and ever in motion. Building a best life requires more than mere motion, and more than mere effort or baby steps. It truly requires enthusiasm, zeal, and zest, along with the unbridled passion discussed in the previous chapter.

Action is for those who are willing to sprint and go all out. There are no half-measures or shortcuts. Each action taken must be considered, measured, and weighed, as each must fit into the larger context of the overall plan.

Success is ultimately the province of the one who is on fire, the one who is utterly determined, and the one who will keep shoveling and shoveling in the resolute belief that he or she will indeed move the mountain placed in his or her path, no matter its girth or its mass.

When you are going all out, fear itself gets cast aside and all systems are go, because the committed, engaged, and utterly active have no time for fear.

Of course, it is you who must implement your plan, as there is no magic in the moonlight out there that will do it for you. Plans are always the wellsprings of action, and, as such, your plan is not made to gather dust.

Action is passion in motion. As Pablo Picasso said, it is "the foundational key to all success."

"Infuse your life with action," proclaimed Bradley Whitford, the actor who played Josh Lyman on the long-running Emmy Award-winning series "The West Wing." He said, "Don't wait for it to happen. Make it happen. Make your own future. Make your own hope. Make your own love. And whatever your belief, honor your creator, not by passively waiting for grace to come down from on high, but by doing what you can to make grace happen."

Or, as Bo Bennett, author of *Year to Success*, writes, "A dream becomes a goal when action is taken towards its achievement." May you make what he says your daily mantra, for your road to success must follow just such a course—from the dream, to the goal, to the action, to the achievement, bit by bit and step by step, inexorably onward, until you can truly exhale, breathe deeply, and smile broadly after having fulfilled what you set out to accomplish. It can take a long, long time, but it's not the time spent that matters. Rather, fulfillment is in the *doing*. That's action.

Living with Attitude

Like purpose, passion, and action, *attitude* is a larger-than-life word. Your attitude is the embodiment of the very way in which you grapple with life. It is the living expression of your acceptance or rejection of what life dishes out to you.

It is your signature, your logo, your mark.

Ralph Marston went so far as to say, "Excellence is not a skill. It is an attitude." John C. Maxwell said, "People may hear your words, but they feel your attitude." So, yes indeed, attitude is one very big word.

To add to this potent litany of quotes about attitude is a popular saying that goes "We can complain because rose bushes have thorns or rejoice because thorn bushes have roses."

Are you positive, upbeat and smiling when you try to succeed at anything, or are you down on the world and predisposed to think in skeptical terms about what is possible? Do you look for the good in people or rather expect to find the worst in them? Do you expect to take without giving or are you rather a "reap what you sow—you only get what you give" type?

Is the cup always half full, or half empty?

If you think that you can take without giving, if you expect the worst from people, if you are generally negative and slow to smile, or predisposed to give less rather than more, then you might want to save yourself the time and effort and put this book aside right now, because success and a best life just might not be your thing.

That is, of course, unless you are willing to do the hard work, and change!

The truth is that you can begin to change your attitude by simply biting your tongue and smiling when it hurts. You are capable of changing and improving the way you behave and act, if you only have the will. Even the worst of attitudes can be made right with a little spit polish, glue, and hand-holding therapy. Believe it or not, no matter how hard or angry, ditching the negative and accenting the positive just might feel good.

Why on earth would you want to hold onto a negative world view and attitude like that anyway?

It was the great American composer Irving Berlin who wrote in his book, *Gathering No Moss: Memoir of a Reluctant World Traveler*, "Life is 10 percent what you make of it and 90 percent how you take it." He weighed in awfully heavily on the attitude side of achievement, as do I.

What I am telling you is that 90 percent of what we are after here is largely the province of the upbeat and daring, the positive and determined, and the smiling and lighthearted. Yes, 90 percent of it is for those who will go forward undaunted, taking the hits and the failings and climbing over the pitfalls and the potholes, and even the occasional quicksand that will be placed in their paths. It is the positive and the upbeat who can deal with the vagaries and surprises of life.

As Charlie taught me, "Never stop moving in the direction of your dream."

Inspired by Charlie: Success Tips

- **You Carry the Great Tools of the Trade:** Success is, most certainly, all about you as you first look to claim your own special place in the world, but understand that as you ascend in the direction that you have chosen, you will likely be invited to change the world along the way. You will be invited to make a difference and leave a mark for good. The extent to which you do so will be correlated to the singular qualities that define you, your work, and your ascension in life. Charlie taught me to be awake and alive to the suffering of others when he said, "You must give in order to truly live. You must give in order to receive." We're talking about the qualities carried that make life worth living in the first place—qualities such as *compassion*, *honor*, and *humility*—the key qualities that Charlie embraced and exemplified in his service to others. The more that you embrace these great tools for living and carry them always in your tool chest, the greater your success and life will be.

Remember what Einstein wrote: "Try not to become a man of success. Rather become a man of value."

🖋 **Ignore Those "Realistic Expectations:** "Your journey to success begins when you take that first cold, hard look at yourself in the mirror and immerse yourself in that Emersonian trip down deep into the depths of your being to assess just who you are, what you're made of, and what you're capable of. You must do this in order to bore into the primordial powers of your passion, and to then set sail in the direction of your dreams, purpose, success, and best life. You may argue that you hold onto realistic expectations. However, you must understand that there are no limits upon those expectations. All limits are, in the end, just artificial creations. It is you who hold them, you who design them, and you who give them their standing and their power. They most certainly do not hold you, as you are the author of this relationship. It is you who render unto them, the power to hold you down. If you are willing to do the work, you can damn well improve and most certainly change for the better. Artificial limits inevitably and always crumble. As John F. Kennedy said, "There are risks and costs to action. But they are far less than the long range risks of comfortable inaction."

🖋 **Keep a Clear Head:** It is you who must act in the living present. Most certainly, there is a course of action for every step you take and for every choice you make. Planning and drawing the map that will lead to your successful life is no small thing. The vision and the end game or culmination of any plan will, in the end, be the culmination of literally tens of thousands of actions, tens of thousands of choices, tens of thousands of steps forward, and tens of thousands of attitudinal responses to both those choices and steps. While we are all emotional beings, and emotion has its place in great endeavors that include becoming successful and fashioning your best life, you must do your level best to keep your emotions in check. Bore into them, understand them, even use them, but do not allow the emotions to override the reasonable.

Your Attitude Is Everything

Remaining positive always and refusing to let despair in is key. Your disposition and the way you carry yourself has everything to do with just how you advance in life. One of the greatest weapons that you possess is your smile. It disarms, it opens doors, it invites and it encourages, so wear yours always, with the exception of those occasions when either bad news is being placed on the table or you are being reprimanded. Stay upbeat and literally wear your commitment to giving your very best always and to delivering the goods on your sleeves. Wear your determination to exceed expectations. When gentleness is warranted, be gentle, and when strength is needed, be strong. When compassion is warranted, be compassionate. Be exactly what a good human being should be.

Be a believer, a force, a friend. All of this and more is manifested in your attitude, in the very way that you carry yourself.

What is in the attitude, of course, is, in the end, what's in you. So if being faithful and good at both your work and with the world matters to you, carry that. In fact, *wear it*. Wear the fact that you are a winner.

Acting Is Difficult

For some, the unveiling of the plan will involve both working and going to school full-time, and for others, it will, for a time, demand working two jobs or even more. Maybe it will demand that you break out of long-established comfort zones in order to go in an entirely new and different direction. And maybe it will entail working with your family to let them know that your actions are going to involve sacrifice on their part and yours, and that there might be times when it is going to be awfully hard to hold all of the pieces together, times that require you to be courageous and to keep the faith.

I know of so many people who had to confront that critical choice of taking a step back in both standing and salary in order to recalibrate and place themselves back on the right road. Every day, somewhere, there is a general manager of a retail store who might take a trainee position in another company for less money, and an office manager who steps down in order to go where she can do more with her technical abilities, and even that rare businessman who is genuinely making it who steps back, breathes deep, takes the hit, and finally enrolls in culinary school.

For so many who have the guts to take the risk to become who and what they were meant to be, less *does*, for a time, become more. It's only that prominent player in their lives that we call "passion" that inevitably forces such reconsideration and such courageous boldness, for it takes guts to move on in an entirely new direction.

The great Johann Wolfgang Van Goethe wrote, "Thinking is easy, acting is difficult, and to put one's thoughts into action is the most difficult thing in the world." True, it can be exceedingly difficult, but it also is the portal that frees you to be you and fulfill your life's highest aspirations.

All over our great country, there are teachers who resign to enter the service industry and service industry professionals who decide that it's time to teach. There also are the occasional high achievers in business who have cathartic experiences that make them want to apply their talents in the nonprofit world.

God bless them, each and every one of them.

Every day, people are rerouting and determining to go down new and different roads as they continue to discover more and more about themselves. And it's all good, so long as their feet eventually get firmly planted where they were destined to be.

Don't Ever Lead with Your Ego

The Book of Proverbs in the Bible states that "pride cometh before a fall," and that is true.

Keep the ego and pride at bay in the workplace and in the company of your peers. Celebrate the work and the achievement, but not yourself. As Thoreau said, "Go quietly in the direction of your dreams." Note that he said quietly, and not loudly.

The guy with the ego so large that he can't get his head through the doorway is never loved by his colleagues. The egotist, all too often, becomes an obstructive rather than a constructive force, and whatever relationships evolve are likely to be unhealthy. This is such a waste, for what you should be after is building the kind of relationships and connections that last for a lifetime.

Charlie knew all of this, and that's why he taught me to remain humble always. It is not about your pride, but rather your purpose, your goals, and your best life fulfilled. As he said, humility is your friend and ego is not.

Keep Your Eyes Open: Think and Find Every Opportunity

Charlie said "look for what others don't see," and he certainly hit the proverbial nail on the head with that. Keep your mind open. Look beyond, look harder and deeper. If you do not look for what is new in each day, so much will pass you by. Opportunities rise up with the dawn just as the sun does, and anything is possible.

It is in the very nature of opportunity to be like this. It is there. It stares you in the face, but you do not always see it. It can be there to be found in some new information that you become aware of, in an email or a message or a text, in a person you just met, in a referral that was just made, in what transpires at a breakfast or luncheon or meeting, in a project or development or a new enterprise in your region that you just become aware of, in an idea that crosses your mind as you sip your morning coffee, and in so much more.

Everybody needs something, and you must look for those opportunities that may be hidden in the nooks and crannies of your field of endeavor. Always ask yourself: Who needs what you have to offer?

It's Much More Than the Job

To work is to survive, and that can be enough for an ordinary or so-so life. But if you want success, comfort and true fulfillment, if you want to put the icing on life's cake, and if you want to be able to celebrate the story of your life, you already know that it has to be about more than the work alone.

Wake up to the simple fact that it is about so much more than the work, more than the job, and more than the ordinary. Extraordinary is about going beyond. It's about maximizing the passion and the purpose, but it also must be about family, faith, and all of the higher order things that comprise a full life.

Be Grateful and Live Gratefully

It is never just about you. Family may root for you, mentors may guide you, and people will be there for you, all along the way. Maybe a handful, or maybe dozens! And later, quite possibly hundreds and still more will be there, supporting and relying on you.

There is no such thing as being "on your own" when you are living your best life.

In the world I walk in, I see people as blessings and even angels in my life. Today, there are literally thousands of names in my contacts database, including past clients who continue to think of me for themselves or people they know. I am grateful to all of them. I never will take their goodness for granted, nor will I ever let them down.

In turn, I strive every day to refer out business when I can, and think of how I can help others. The more you help others, the more life will reward you.

You can take this to the bank: humility, goodness, character, and reverence also are among the mighty byproducts of true success.

Acknowledge That Nothing Is Final

As you combine your action and attitude, acknowledge that here are no limits and no ends. There are only new beginnings. There are and never have been any final victories. The journey always goes on, just as your pursuit of your best life always goes on.

You may have climbed to the top of your mountain, but there will always be other mountains to climb.

High achievers are never fully satisfied. The day may come when you switch gears, and, while you may redirect your energies, you will never stop achieving. You may bob and weave and adjust, but you keep breathing by going forward, continuing to ascend, and doing more.

No, there are no final victories. "Success is not final, failure is not fatal: It is the courage to continue that counts," said Winston Churchill. That "courage to continue" never abandons one who lives a best life.

The More Joyful, the More Successful

Joy may be the most important attitude of all. The ancient Egyptians had a profound belief about one's entry into heaven. In short, the right to pass into heaven depended on the answer given to two simple questions:

Have you found joy in your life?

Has your life brought joy to others?

That was the only test that one had to pass in order to enter the portal to eternal bliss. There were no questions about success or high achievement or changing the world, but rather two questions about joy and whether or not you found it and passed it on.

Wow, isn't that something! Just joy!

Therefore, be joyful. Find the joy in what you do and prosper and pass your joy unto others. Should you find the joy in what you do—and how can you not if you are following your heart in the pursuit of purpose and passion—you will succeed all the more. If you do, you will be an unstoppable force. The actual truth is that there will be joy enough in the mere pursuit of meshing vocation and avocation.

Write the Story of Your Life

It doesn't matter if it's a sentence, a paragraph, fifty pages, or a book. Writing the story of your life and addressing what you want to be remembered for is a telling and often game-changing exercise. It forces you to imagine and envision. It forces you to construct your best possible plan and, maybe, just maybe, to replace the one that you originally cobbled together.

This exercise is designed to help you distill purpose and passion to its essence. It shines a bright light upon just who and what you are and, most especially, upon just who and what you aim to be. It makes you a believer again. It gives you faith. It gets you back on track.

And yes, you are always free to rewrite.

I think about you writing your own story, and I hear this great line of Leonardo Da Vinci, who accomplished more than enough for one hundred lifetimes. He wrote, "It had long since come to my attention that people of accomplishment rarely sat back and let things happen to them. They went out and happened to things."

Happen to things—write your story and make it happen.

Twenty-Four Hours and Limitless Resources

Every day, you are given 24 precious hours, and it is up to you to use each one as best you can. Each day will be comprised of choices and actions. You will establish and determine the pace. There's no rocket science, of course, in suggesting that the faster the pace, the faster the climb. That's it, no less and no more. You get the same 24 hours every single new and promising day. Use them wisely. Be willing to do justice to each hour, be a doer and not a slacker, and you will steadfastly advance in the direction of your dreams.

It helps a great deal to know that you are armed with so many extraordinary tools today. You are living in the height of a historic age of technological advancement, where new apps, bringing you ever closer to all knowledge and information and people, get spit out by the game-changers weekly. Microsoft and Apple and the internet and Google and all the rest have made this amazing world so much smaller. No matter the interest or field of endeavor that inspires you, your exploration of it is but the snap of a fingertip away.

The opportunity to self-educate has never been greater, the very thought of which, given the theme of this chapter, reminds me of the words of Herbert Spencer, one of the Victorian era's great philosophers and political theorists. He wrote, "The great aim of education is not knowledge but action."

What he wrote is simply extraordinary, and it speaks loudly to what we are about here. More than 125 years ago, he hit the nail on the head by suggesting that education itself is but the rudimentary foundation of action, and that it is the "acting upon" what you have learned that ultimately counts.

Knowledge for knowledge's sake is of no value.

It is only, he affirms, the acting upon knowledge that has intrinsic value.

By the way, let me also note that the internet presents you with an opportunity to take your own "career aptitude" tests and your own "values clarification" tests, tools in that most essential effort to pinpoint just what your true avocation and purpose is. Of course, it is you who must take the journey within and you who ultimately calls the shots on your behalf, but it's nice to know, via tests such as these, that some fairly astute psychologists can, at least, weigh in on your behalf.

Mixing It Up to Find Joy and Grace

There's also something to be said for not doing the exact same thing day after day. It's good to keep things interesting, so shaking up or tweaking the schedule and the routine makes a lot of sense. It's also extremely important to take at least 10 minutes out of each day for quiet reflection and consideration, for looking inside and taking a personal litmus test.

Take 10 minutes to ask yourself questions like: *Am I where I want to be? What more, if anything, can I do? What happened yesterday or today that I can do more with? Who can help me? Where do I turn next?* This goes a long way in helping you become better, so I strongly suggest that you make it a habit to pointedly take out ten minutes each day for introspection, and when used wisely, I promise you that these 10 minutes will become the most important minutes of your days.

The author of the classic book *The Little Prince* once wrote, "It is in the compelling zest of high adventure and of victory, and in creative action, that man finds his supreme joys." Creative action, he insisted, evokes the supreme joys. Wow! Others have already told us, in no uncertain terms, that action can be an almost profound instrument of grace.

Out of action, out of doing, out of your motion, there exists the exciting prospect of fashioning both joy and grace, which excites me.

So many spend too much time wishing that they were different—a little old attitudinal response mechanism called jealousy, which never gives way to anything constructive and can often prove to be utterly destructive.

There's also an awful lot of anger that often gets directed at those who highly succeed—anger that gets tossed around rather indiscriminately. It gets voiced in envious, unkind comments such as, "Can you *believe* how successful he/she is or what he/she is doing?" Again, just in case there's any doubt, this is but another regressive force that only represses the one who voices it, and never takes that person the slightest bit higher.

The truth is that you'll go much further admiring them and, to whatever degree possible, studying and trying to emulate their success, rather than despising them.

Rethinking Action and Attitude

Your attitude is everything. It is who you are. Our old friend Winston Churchill referred to attitude as "the little thing that makes a big difference," and the bigger difference is always whether that attitude is positive or negative.

Accordingly, as it was once often said, "A bad attitude is like a flat tire. If you don't change it, you'll never go anywhere."

If you were to google synonyms for action, among the many you would find would be force, life, movement, plan, bustle, dash, going, happening, motion, power, vigor, vitality, and spirit. That's not a bad bunch of words with which to go to battle with, when the battle is for your dreams, your success, and your best life.

It is about doing, moving, plotting, finishing, daring, and achieving. If you are not up and doing, one of two things has probably happened: You are either stuck in the mud, or you are about to fall off the cliff's edge into the great abyss.

Jack Canfield, the originator of the famous *Chicken Soup for the Soul* book series, wrote, "Successful people maintain a positive focus in life no matter what is going on around them. They stay focused on their past successes rather than their past failures, and on the next action steps they need to take to get them closer to the fulfillment of their goals, rather than all the other distractions life presents to them."

Each action taken, each step forward, and each movement will generate an attitudinal response that affects actions to come. Simply know this: The mind never rests. Be it rationally, or emotionally, it never stops judging, evaluating, weighing, and forcefully suggesting. It can sure pump up the adrenaline and give way to either anger or acceptance. Again, it is your job to stay in control of this process.

As to attitude, the synonyms are equally telling. They include stance, posture, viewpoint, outlook, perspective, standpoint, position, temper, temperament, inclination, orientation, reaction, and approach. Each action you take activates or puts in play all of these telling synonyms of attitude.

In what we do and what we think about what we do, our lives are lived.

It is a huge and extraordinary process that you must consciously and vigilantly engage. As the great Zig Ziglar, author and motivational speaker, has said, "It is your attitude and not your aptitude that determines your altitude." The truth is that, while what you know is critically important, he argues in this profound statement that how you live your life and how you respond to it are even more important.

What Would Charlie Say?

Charlie believed with all his heart in the importance of action and attitude. He firmly believed that opportunities present themselves to all, but that they are fully maximized only by those who determine to go after them. As he told me, "There is so much opportunity out there. Go after whatever you want in life and give it your all."

I have shared enough words and thoughts about action and attitude, their importance, and the symbiotic relationship between the two. Still, I have one more philosophical contribution from Rainer Maria Rilke, a powerful and moving Austrian poet of the late nineteenth and early twentieth century.

Rilke wrote:

How should we be able to forget those ancient myths that are at the beginning of all peoples, the myths about dragons that at the last moment turn into princesses; perhaps all the dragons of our lives are princesses who are only waiting to see us once beautiful and brave. Perhaps everything terrible is in deepest being something helpless that only wants help from us.

So you must not be frightened if a sadness rises up before you larger than any you have ever seen; if a restiveness, like light and cloud shadows, passes over your hands and over all you do. You must think that something is happening with you, that life has not forgotten you, that it holds you in its hand; it will not let you fall. Why do you want to shut out of your life any uneasiness, any miseries, or any depressions? For after all, you do not know what work these conditions are doing inside you.

Indeed, this is not a bad way to look at your life, and at all of the trials, tribulations, and doubts that your own actions may evoke. Yes, it is about your actions, the actions of all those who affect you, and your responses to both. Rilke suggests that everything, the bad as well as the good, happens for a reason, and that even that which is most difficult and entirely unwanted still teaches and instructs and enlightens, rendering you richer and stronger in the end.

Before you run and hide, he seems to say, let wisdom take a first crack at that which troubles.

Be up and doing, but consider each action and corresponding reaction. Even more importantly, consider your attitudinal responses to the same, which have everything to do with how you will likely act the next day.

Be up and doing, be daring, be bold, be aware, and be vigilant. In the ways that we've discussed, action and attitude will get you far.

4

The Nature of Success

"Don't look back. You are not going that way."
— Unknown

"Be resilient, persevere, and never give up on yourself."
"To work is to survive and that can be enough."
"There are no limits and no ends."
— Charlie

Success is the result of passion and purpose. When action, attitude, contribution, and service are added to the mix, it may result in the achievement of the desired goals and in the fulfillment of your dreams. However, keep in mind that success can be more of a moving target than a finish line. It's a process in which you take steps forward each and every day.

And while there may not be any final victories or grand slams, there is a measure of success, genuine success, in the pursuit alone—in the stepping up to the plate day after day, in never quitting on yourself or on those you love, or in the nobility or honor to be found in the purpose that is being pursued or served. As such, there is also something special to be realized in the small victories and in living a better life for having dared to dream.

Success is relative, and it comes in many different ways, shapes, sizes, and guises. It is rarely, if ever, absolute. Look around and ask yourself, who among the most successful in the world has quit? The greatest achievers and the most successful don't quit. Final curtain calls, ends, and pure retirements are rare indeed, as the bugle never stops summoning the masses of dream catchers, inviting them to extend themselves further.

Where fear and self-doubt sets in, all bets are off, for if you succumb to those feelings, they will inhibit or potentially prevent your success. If you don't believe in yourself, who on earth will? Pride also corrupts the pursuit of success, as does a sense of entitlement. As Charlie understood so well, the world owes you nothing; it is you, as a matter of fact, who owes the world. A lack of goodness, compassion, decency, and honesty also corrupts the process, and leaves all too many dangling and frayed edges.

All of this notwithstanding, it is, in the end (as I have already written again and again) your call. If you want it bad enough, and you are willing to be relentless in the pursuit, and you are willing to make the sacrifices that it takes, then there is no power or force on earth to stand in your way.

Get the education, the training, the knowledge, and the skills that it takes. Embrace your passion and your purpose. Identify your mentors. Draw up the plan that will no doubt be refined again and again. Begin and act accordingly. Pray. Develop winning habits. Maintain a positive attitude. Be patient, be kind, and serve others. Stay on course or correct your course. Reach out to your mentor. Execute your ideas as the years pass. Have faith, be honest, and be good to all those in your circle. Correct your course again. Volunteer and get out of yourself. Measure the progress. Enjoy a few more years of growth and development—more years, more grit, more patience, more growth, the crisis of faith—and sometime on someday, you'll realize that you did what you set out to do.

It may even catch you off guard and surprise you, but there you will be, bowing your head in thanks, celebrating the ascension and manifestation of your purpose and passion. You will have done what you set out to do and there it will be, staring you in the face—the very life that you long ago imagined.

All of this comes with a catch: Once you have worked so hard for so long, hard work becomes a habit, and you're more than likely going to go right on working just as hard as ever.

The pursuit of the prize gets into the blood.

Success truly is never an accident. It is always a choice.

It is just that simple. To succeed, you must choose to be successful. So do it. Make the choice to be successful, and make it as soon as possible.

Determining that you are going to be successful, and incorporating that mindset into what you think and what you do every day of your life is critical. You must chart out your personal plan and you must advance in that direction religiously.

Your first steps involve setting out to become the expert in your field, and it is incumbent upon you to gather all of the knowledge and information that you will need. There are no shortcuts here, as knowledge is essential, and you will go nowhere without it. The more expert you are, the more keys you possess with which to unlock the future.

Success is your right and your province. Believe that, advance in that direction always, and you will, I promise, live successfully. Just stay the course and keep anxiety and fear on the shelf where they belong. Don't ever treat negativity with respect, for it is your enemy and is not worthy of you.

As you implement your plan, in order to be truly successful in life you must remember to live, learn, love, laugh, and be a force for good who shares this bounty with others.

Only You Can Guarantee Success

As I noted in Chapter 1, thousands of players in the success trade will promise you that if you read their book, watch their videos, listen to their programs, or come to their workshops, you will succeed—"no muss, no fuss," absolutely guaranteed.

If only that were true. In the real world, the guarantee of success can only come from you.

You are the sole guarantor in your life.

You decide. You determine. You plan. You implement. You affect. All of it is up to you, as you and you alone get to place the guaranteed stamp upon your work.

Of course, as I noted earlier, it might help you to know that our dear friend Dr. Seuss believed in you. "So be sure when you step," he wrote. "Step with care and great tact. And remember that life's a great balancing act. And will you succeed? Yes! You will, indeed! 98 and ¾ percent guaranteed!"

Real Life Lessons on What It Takes to Achieve Success

Scott Smith had the kind of parents who never stopped telling him that he could do anything, the kind who filled his cup with self-worth and self-confidence. An accomplished journalist and author, he set out to do his bit to raise others up, and certainly succeeded in that effort with his highly acclaimed book, *Extraordinary People: Real Life Lessons on What It Takes to Achieve Success*. Drawing on his experience as an entrepreneur and business reporter, he set out to find the common traits, or common denominators and behaviors, that were manifested by successful luminaries from all walks of life.

The prominent traits that he found included *courage, fearlessness, the willingness to make dramatic change or to risk, optimism, faith in human capacity, an innovative imagination, and a dogged persistence in the face of adversity.* While learning what allowed them to reach enduring success, the reader also learns about their lives and their contributions.

Those featured included the American rhythm and blues icon Ray Charles; Martha Harper, inventor of the franchise system; Simon Bolivar, the liberator of six South American nations; Anne Rice, the novelist; Antoine de Saint-Exupery, the author of *The Little Prince*; Reed Hastings, CEO of Netflix; Jim Henson, the creator of the Muppets; John F. Kennedy, the 35th President of the United States; Catherine the Great, the Empress of Russia; Stephen Hawking, the physicist; General Douglas MacArthur; John Quincy Adams, the sixth president of the United States; Jackie Joyner Kersey, Olympic athlete; and Quincy Jones, music producer. What an extraordinary and diverse array of the highest of achievers!

Scott wrote, "I took an in-depth look at people past and present, who I admire. Human nature hasn't changed a lot since the cave man days; we just have more tools and toys, so historical figures can shed light on our current circumstances. The difference between success and failure is often just a matter of psychology, so we need their inspiration."

Ultimately, Scott proclaims this clear and simple mantra:

Be prepared. Change course. Be courageous. Communicate smartly. Act audaciously. Be a team player. Be nice, finish first. Maintain integrity. Create something new.

"What makes the desert beautiful," said Saint-Exupery's Little Prince, "is that somewhere it hides a well." Like the man wandering in the desert in search of salvation, one who wanders on the long and winding road that leads to a best life must also find the well that is hidden, the prize that unlocks and unravels all the vagaries and mysteries.

The Daily Success Habits of Wealthy People

Thomas Corley, author of *Rich Habits: The Daily Success Habits of Wealthy Individuals*, understands the difference between being rich and poor all too well. At the tender age of nine, his family went from living the life of multimillionaires to becoming flat broke in just one night.

To write this profound and telling study, Corley observed and documented the daily activities of 233 wealthy people and 128 people living in poverty for five years. He discovered that there is a tremendous difference between the habits of the wealthy and the poor. In fact, his research revealed more than 200 daily activities that separated the "haves" from the "have-nots." The culmination of his detailed work can be found in his bestselling book, but I take the liberty of sharing just twenty of his compelling findings. *Res Ipsa Loquitor*, it is said in the Latin, for the thing indeed speaks for itself.

- 70 percent of the wealthy eat less than 300 junk food calories per day. 97 percent of poor people eat more than 300 junk food calories per day.

- 23 percent of the wealthy gamble. 52 percent of poor people gamble.

- 80 percent of the wealthy are focused on accomplishing some single goal. Only 12 percent of the poor do this.

- 76 percent of the wealthy exercise aerobically four days a week. 23 percent of the poor do this.

- 63 percent of the wealthy listen to audio books during commute to work vs. 5 percent of poor people.
- 81 percent of the wealthy maintain a to-do list vs. 19 percent of the poor.
- 63 percent of wealthy parents make their children read two or more non-fiction books a month vs. 3 percent of the poor.
- 70 percent of wealthy parents make their children volunteer 10 hours or more per month vs. 3 percent of the poor.
- 80 percent of the wealthy make "happy birthday" calls vs. 11 percent of the poor.
- 67 percent of the wealthy write down their goals vs. 17 percent of the poor.
- 88 percent of the wealthy read 30 minutes or more each day for education or career reasons vs. 2 percent of the poor.
- 6 percent of the wealthy say what's on their mind vs. 69 percent of the poor.
- 79 percent of the wealthy network five hours or more each month vs. 16 percent of the poor.
- 67 percent of the wealthy watch one hour or less of TV every day vs. 23 percent of the poor.
- 6 percent of the wealthy watch reality TV vs. 78 percent of the poor.
- 44 percent of the wealthy wake up three hours before work starts vs. 3 percent of the poor.
- 74 percent of the wealthy teach good daily success habits to their children vs. 1 percent of the poor.
- 84 percent of the wealthy believe good habits create opportunity vs. 4 percent of the poor.

- 76 percent of the wealthy believe bad habits generate detrimental luck vs. 9 percent of the poor.

- 86 percent of the wealthy believe in lifelong educational self-improvement vs. 5 percent of the poor.

- 86 percent of the wealthy love to read vs. 26 percent of the poor.

These contrasting habits are stark and overwhelming. They demand that government, society, and community intervene with public educational and social policies that address the profound and pressing disadvantage faced by the poor. Habits form, evolve, and become ingrained. This must change. Good habits must be developed, or generations will be lost.

Every single one of Corley's findings suggest that the wealthy take care of themselves and their families, and that they look to improve and advance, while the poor simply do not. Ultimately, *Rich Habits* is, to me, a call to action.

We have discussed the need for anyone who aspires to succeed to develop good habits. See what the fortunate wealthy do above, and then do the same. Treat your body, your mind and your spirit with all the care, tenderness and love that they deserve. Take care, improve, never stop growing, and then succeed.

Striving for a Better Life

Like most people, David Singer has strived mightily to make his life better. Unlike so many people, he has learned to improve his life in hundreds of ways while avoiding the stress, frustration, and guilt that can follow the failed attempts at making meaningful and lasting change via New Year's resolutions. "We have all been there," he writes, "looking at a largely unchanged list a year later." And the year after that, and so on and so forth!

Singer has much to offer, but I found myself focusing on his *Simple Ways to Give Back and Help Others Starting Today*. Singer is fascinating in that he believes the most vital habit that one can develop in order to become successful is to first become a *giver*. A giver of resources, sure, but most importantly, he believes that great benefits will flow back to you.

Saint Francis' Prayer of Peace goes, "For it is in the pardoning that we are pardoned and in the giving that we receive." Singer takes this to the bank.

You can't help but love him and his relentless commitment to what he sees as a compelling truth. He quotes Winston Churchill saying, "We make a living by what we get, but we make a life by what we give."

He argues that you should become involved in community and charitable service, and he urges you to make it a family and friend thing, which will be even more enriching. Besides, giving is enjoyable, and it has proven to be good for your health and your happiness. Studies have clearly shown that people who volunteer live longer. How's that for an incentive?

You get to embrace a passion, and you get the opportunity to get out of your own head and your own worries. Giving helps you focus on the faithful essentials of life, and not just your personal needs or selfishness. Studies also show that those who give of themselves and who are of service to others are far less likely to suffer from anxiety or depression.

Singer wrote, "I recently heard it said (by a politician, of all people) that if you preach to the choir, they will sing, and I want us to sing. I want you to tell everyone you know about the importance and benefit, of giving to others." For Singer, it seemed that giving had become his own Holy Grail. If succeeding in life is your goal, he loudly proclaims, giving of yourself to others must come first. It is the primary portal to goodness, fulfillment, and anyone's best life.

More Authors Weigh In on Success

Yvette Long's book, *Aspire to Excellence*, is wholly focused on initiatives and immersion programs for troubled and at risk teens. Indeed her book has evolved into an Aspire to Excellence clinic, what is now an intervention program for at risk teens headquartered in Chester, New Jersey. "God has given each of us unique talents and gifts," Long writes, "but the challenge is to recognize, appreciate and, with confidence, utilize them to make our world a better place in which to live. Within this discovery lies true success."

Being a teenager means constantly trying to figure out who you are, what you're good at, and what you want to do with your life. Every day brings new challenges and new questions. Long writes that *Aspire to Excellence* is about how we respond in helping young men to take more of a leadership role in their lives and to develop the self-confidence to realize their dreams.

Phil Spillane's *Starting with the Destination in Mind: How to Create Wealth in Any Economy* is largely an investment, wealth management, and wealth development tome. In sharing personal experiences and in relying on insights derived from notables such as Ben Franklin, Steve Jobs, and even the beloved Yogi Berra, Spillane manages to take a subject that would otherwise be tedious and make it user friendly. He comes off as the friend from the neighborhood who sits across the kitchen table from you who is simply never at a loss for words.

Robert Gignac's *Your Richly Imagined Future* explores basic financial concepts from goal-setting to risk management to wills, yet a considerable slice of his book is dedicated to work-life balance, quality of life, and personal motivation issues. It is the focus on concepts such as these that distinguishes this effort and separates it from others in this genre.

Charlie taught me to be resilient and never give up on myself. This lesson is exemplified in Nadine Lajoie's *Win the Race of Life...with Balance and*

Passion at 180 MPH. This story fascinates because of Nadine's past life in the male-dominated world of motorcycle competition, including her third-place finish in a field of 75 men at Daytona in 2007. Once ranked among the Top 10 winners of the National WERA Championship, Nadine keeps busy today "IN-Powering others to overcome their fears and RACE toward their dreams."

Win the Race of Life blends adrenaline, power and success with life lessons. Nadine's mantras are to: *Focus on the dream, develop the mindset of a champion, tap adrenaline, tap passion, exercise discipline, never give up, get it done, get out of your comfort zone, and maintain the all-out energy input.* A strong and determined woman, she loves the pursuit of success itself. One senses that there will be no end game for her.

Inspired by Charlie: Success Tips

- **Respond to people as quickly as possible.** This is what I like to call my "rapid response formula," and it is truly one of the primary secrets to my success. The faster you respond to people, the more highly they will think of you. The formula is simple, and it suggests that you both value and respect them. I love overly impressing anyone who emails or texts me. I try to respond within minutes, if not seconds, when they send me a message. Whenever someone asks me a question for which I don't have an answer, I don't ever guess. If I am not 100 percent sure of the answer, I just say that I will do the research and get back to them. Most importantly, always, always, *always*, do what you say that you are going to do. In the classic book, *The Four Agreements*, the first of the four is to "be impeccable with your word." So value people, respect them, respond to them at the speed of light, tell them the truth always, and do excellent work. If you do, you will never lose them and they will be a referral lightning rod for you.

- **On the way up, try to live below your means.** To live below your means is another secret to becoming a success in life, for when you do that, you will never be stressed about paying the bills and you'll know that you have the extra money set aside for the emergencies and the unexpected. So, try, try, try, to live low, unless and until you are able to live high. Too many people are caught up with having the big house, the big car, the expensive watch, the fancy clothes, and all the fine trappings. How about not worrying about all of that and buying only what you can afford, paying your bills on time, and spending more time with your family and friends on those precious things that don't necessarily cost the big bucks.

- **Leverage everything.** I love the line, "live, love, learn, and laugh." But I like to add the word "leverage" in there as well. My point is that you must leverage everything you have in order to gain ground as you ascend on your path. I'm talking about leveraging your relationships, your abilities, your skills, your personality, your likability factor, your passion, your drive. All of it! Use everything in your arsenal. It is what will separate you from your competition. There is only one you, and you can determine to be better than the rest.

- **Develop speaking skills.** Learning to speak, make professional presentations, and effectively market yourself matters a great deal because it sets you apart and automatically places you on a higher level. Stepping up to be a panelist at workshops, and stepping further still to confront full audiences, distinguishes you. Naturally, it is very important that you be able to converse with anyone about what you do and how you do it. You should have your own 30-second commercial burned into your brain, and you should be certain that it comes off as very informative and to the point. There are organizations like Toastmasters and Dale Carnegie, where you can get assistance if need be, but know this truth: Anyone with a head on their shoulders who knows what they do and who they are can speak. So put the fear aside and do so.

- **Be the expert.** Learn, learn, learn, and never stop learning until you become your industry's standard. Be the expert in your field, be the best, be the exception, be the one that people turn to for answers when they don't have them. At the very least, never stop aspiring to be the best, and that means never stop planning your work, working your plan, and to never forget that anything worth doing is worth doing extremely well.

Seven People Who Changed the World

As discussed already in this chapter, you can learn a great deal from those who have walked the talk—who transported themselves to the pinnacle of success. Charlie said, "To work is to survive and that can be enough," and that is most certainly true. However, he also taught me that "there are no limits and no ends." That's also true, and very good things can come to those who embrace the initial principle of hard work. Here are a few of my personal success models.

ABRAHAM LINCOLN, 16TH PRESIDENT OF THE UNITED STATES

Abraham Lincoln's will and genius alone saved our Union, preserved government "of, by, and for the people," emancipated the slaves, and ended 300 years of gross and harsh injustice.

He did all of this, and much more, by bringing disparate and estranged groups together, and forming fragile coalitions that were bound by the sheer force of his will. That same will also subdued the peace movement.

But Lincoln is ever so much more than the warrior or redeemer president. No leader in our country was a better communicator or writer than he. His philosophy and world view are preserved in speeches, proclamations, and letters, penned in a day when presidents didn't require hundreds of staff members to do their writing for them.

All of Lincoln's words were his words.

And yes indeed, he often shared thoughts on success, achievement, leadership and how best to advance in life. What follows is a sampling of my favorites.

> "I am not bound to win, but I am bound to be true. I am not bound to succeed, but I am bound to live by the light that I have. I must stand with anybody that stands right, and stand with him while he is right, and part with him when he goes wrong. I am bound to be true and bound to live by the light I have. Should one's morals, values, and principles be tossed in order to succeed, there is no true success, for the life itself is corrupted, diminished and impoverished. All the money in the world, maybe, but there will be no joy in the land."

> "Give me six hours to chop down a tree and I will spend the first four sharpening the axe."

"Always bear in mind that your own resolution to succeed is more important than any other."

"I'm a slow walker, but I never walk back."

"The best thing about the future is that it comes one day at a time."

"Leave nothing for tomorrow which can be done today."

"Your own resolution to succeed is more important than any other."

"In the end, it's not the years in your life that count. It's the life in your years."

"The best way to predict the future is to create it!"

HENRY DAVID THOREAU, NATURALIST AND PHILOSOPHER

Henry David Thoreau was a naturalist, a transcendental philosopher, and a great believer in human possibility, providence, and purpose. The author of *Walden* and *Civil Disobedience* urged people to simplify their lives, dream big, and be true to their values and convictions, no matter the cost.

When he lay dying of tuberculosis at the age of 45, it is said that one of his loving and pious aunts whispered to him, "Henry, have you made your peace with God." Upon hearing that, it is said that he opened his eyes one last time and said, "I was never aware of the fact that we had ever had a quarrel." What a way to go out! His final words were a lesson for us all to be faithful, honorable, and true.

When life allows, anyone who hasn't had the pleasure should take some time with *Walden, Civil Disobedience,* and *Life on the Concord and Merrimack Rivers.* Outside of the essay, his work can be read in pieces, a couple of pages at a time. Dead for more than 150 years, he still lives in his words—and they are words that can only enrich your life.

While he never set out to give motivational speeches or to write thesis about success, the natural inclination he had to address the essentials and the meaning of life sure brought him into the field. Here is a sampling of his profound and powerful thinking.

> "If one advances confidently in the direction of his dreams, and endeavors to live the life which he has imagined, he will meet with a success unexpected in common hours."

> "It's not what you look at that matters, it's what you see."

> "Dreams are the touchstones of our characters."

> "Never look back unless you are planning to go that way."

> "Most men lead lives of quiet desperation and go to the grave with the song still in them."

> "What lies behind us and what lies ahead of us are tiny matters compared to what lives within us."

> "You must live in the present, launch yourself on every wave, find your eternity in each moment. Fools stand on their island of opportunities and look toward another land. There is no other land; there is no other life but this."

> "If a man does not keep pace with his companions, perhaps it is because he hears a different drummer. Let him step to the music he hears, however measured or far away."

> "If you have built castles in the air, your work need not be lost; that is where they should be. Now put the foundations under them."

RALPH WALDO EMERSON, AMERICA'S PHILOSOPHER

Ralph Waldo Emerson was an American poet, essayist, and philosopher who maintained a profound and highly romantic belief in the power of the individual to move mountains and fulfill dreams. He challenged traditional thinking, railed against hypocrisy, and urged people to first journey within before ever attempting to journey without.

Emerson's essay "Nature" (1836) is perhaps the best expression of his transcendentalism, the belief that everything in our world—even a drop of dew on the grass or a windshield—is a microcosm of the entire universe. "Trust thyself" was his motto and his mantra, and his relentless faith in the capacity of each and every human being is manifested in his essays and poems.

Ever the optimist, he was a believer in the "divine sufficiency of the individual." (Some of you may also know Emerson for his, "By the rude bridge that arched the flood.")

Here are a few of my favorite Emerson quotes:

> *"The good news is that the moment you decide that what you know is more important than what you have been taught to believe, you will have shifted gears in your quest for abundance. Success comes from within, not from without."*

> *"Finish each day and be done with it. You have done what you could. Some blunders and absurdities no doubt crept in; forget them as soon as you can. Tomorrow is a new day. You shall begin it serenely and with too high a spirit to be encumbered with your old nonsense."*

> *"Always do what you are afraid to do."*

> *"Do not go where the path may lead, go instead where there is no path and leave a trail."*

"The purpose of life is not to be happy. It is to be useful, to be honorable, to be compassionate, to have it make some difference that you have lived and lived well."

"Whatever you do, you need courage. Whatever course you decide upon, there is always someone to tell you that you are wrong. There are always difficulties arising that tempt you to believe your critics are right. To map out a course of action and follow it to an end requires some of the same courage that a soldier needs. Peace has its victories, but it takes brave men and women to win them."

"Dare to live the life you have dreamed for yourself. Go forward and make your dreams come true."

"It is not the length of life, but the depth."

"The only person you are destined to become is the person you decide to be."

"Life is a journey, not a destination."

"Cultivate the habit of being grateful for every good thing that comes to you, and to give thanks continuously. And because all things have contributed to your advancement, you should include all things in your gratitude."

STEVE JOBS, FOUNDER OF APPLE

In 1976, Steve Jobs, at the tender age of 21, along with his friend, Steve Wozniak, gave life to Apple Computer. His parents had given him up at birth and he had been adopted. He was that familiar prankster and troublemaker in school, the type whose future promise is always questioned. Initially, he underachieved, but he tested so well that it was scary. This speaks well for all of you out there who may have been labeled as a problem child in the earliest of your days. (Just for the record, they had given up on Einstein as well.)

The Nature of Success

Wozniak and Jobs both loved electronics, and they funded their entrepreneurial venture by Jobs selling his Volkswagen bus and Wozniak selling his beloved scientific calculator. Together, these two young men revolutionized the computer industry by democratizing the technology and making the machines smaller, cheaper, more intuitive, and accessible to everyday consumers.

Six years into their venture, that Volkswagen and calculator had given rise to an empire worth $1.2 billion. They floundered a bit later but rose back up with the Macintosh before Jobs left in 1985.

In 1986, Jobs purchased the digital animation company Pixar from George Lucas and gave us *Toy Story*, *Finding Nemo*, *The Incredibles*, and other fantastic films. Netting $4 billion, there was a historic merger when Pixar joined the wonderful world of Walt Disney. This, by the way, made Jobs Disney's largest shareholder. He returned to Apple in 1997 and is credited with revitalizing the company and driving the evolution of the technology that drives our world, from iTunes to the iPad to the iPod.

A rare genius and a digital visionary, Steve Jobs changed the world. Few of us out there, of course, are destined to achieve as mightily as this genius, but, as he so often said, everyone is capable of succeeding, contributing, and making a difference. The "master evangelist of the digital age" died at home with his family in Palo Alto, California in 2011.

So what did Jobs say about success?

> *"I'm convinced that about half of what separates successful people from the non-successful ones is pure perseverance."*

> *"Have the courage to follow your heart and intuition. They somehow know what you truly want to become."*

> *"Let's go invent tomorrow rather than worrying about what happened yesterday."*

"If today were the last day of your life, would you want to do what you are about to do today?"

"Your work is going to fill a large part of your life, and the only way to be truly satisfied is to do what you believe is great work. And the only way to do great work is to love what you do. If you haven't found it yet, keep looking. Don't settle. As with all matters of the heart, you'll know when you find it."

"We don't get a chance to do that many things, and everyone should be really excellent. Because this is our life. Life is brief, and then you die, you know? And we've all chosen to do this with our lives. So it better be damn good. It better be worth it."

"You can't connect the dots looking forward; you can only connect them looking backward. So you have to trust that the dots will somehow connect in your future. You have to trust in something—your gut, destiny, life and karma, whatever. This approach has never let me down, and it has made all the difference in my life."

"My model for business is The Beatles. They were four guys who kept each other's kind of negative tendencies in check. They balanced each other, and the total was greater than the sum of the parts. That's how I see business: Great things in business are never done by one person, they're done by a team of people."

"Do you want to spend the rest of your life selling sugared water or do you want to change the world?"

"Do your best work. No shortcuts. No excuses. Be more perfect and exacting than anyone else. Your best work, your very best, every single day of your life."

BILLS GATES OF MICROSOFT AND THE BILL & MELINDA GATES FOUNDATION

Who out there—anywhere out there—hasn't heard of Bill Gates, the primary founder of Microsoft, who today has set his eyes upon curing the grave illnesses and problems that plague the underdeveloped world?

Gates and Paul Allen had what you call "that vision thing," and what they saw was the opportunity to start their own computer software company. Gates dropped out of Harvard, began with nothing but the ideas in his head, and proceeded to drive the very future of computer technology and its vital operating systems forward. Today, anyone with a dream or an idea and a computer has long been familiar with Microsoft. It has become a part of the very language we speak.

Today, Gates is among the richest people on the planet. Between 2009 and 2014 alone, his wealth more than doubled from $40 billion to more than $82 billion. By 2022 Forbes estimated that he was the fourth-richest person in the world, worth a staggering $129 billion. One of the very best entrepreneurs in living history, he faced many challenges and court cases that decried his company as anti-competitive, but, despite the storms and public rebukes, they did experience remarkable growth and success.

In 2000 Gates left Microsoft to pursue his philanthropic endeavors full time, forming the Bill & Melinda Gates foundation with his former wife. Soon joined by another extraordinary entrepreneur, Warren Buffett, by 2020 it was the second largest charitable foundation in the world, holding $49.8 billion in assets. The foundation has committed to paying out $9 billion annually by 2026. Tackling worldwide problems like malaria, HIV, world hunger, extreme poverty, community sanitation, clean water access, and more, they are, as I write this, on a mission, to change lives and our world for the better.

With Buffett's help, "We were able to be unbelievably ambitious," Gates said, and that is indeed what they are. Everyone who cares about the wellbeing of the human race owes them a debt of gratitude. Gates, too, has thoughts to offer you on the nature of success. Here are a few more of his thoughts:

> "I really had a lot of dreams when I was a kid, and I think a great deal of that grew out of the fact that I had a chance to read a lot."

> "Don't compare yourself with anyone in this world. If you do so, you are insulting yourself."

> "Patience is a key element of success."

> "Flipping burgers is not beneath your dignity. Your grandparents had a different word for burger flipping–they called it opportunity."

> "Our success has really been based on partnerships from the very beginning."

> "The world won't care about your self-esteem. The world will expect you to accomplish something BEFORE you feel good about yourself."

> "This is a fantastic time to be entering the business world, because business is going to change more in the next 10 years than it has in the last 50."

> "It's fine to celebrate success, but it is more important to heed the lessons of failure."

> "If I'd had some set idea of a finish line, don't you think I would have crossed it years ago?"

> "To win big, you sometimes have to take big risks."

The Nature of Success

JEFF BEZOS OF AMAZON.COM

The third-richest person in the world (net worth: $124.3 billion), entrepreneur and e-commerce pioneer Jeff Bezos had an early love of computers and studied computer science and electrical engineering at Princeton University. In 1994, at the age of 30, he quit a lucrative job to test the untapped potential of the internet market by opening Amazon.com, the virtual bookstore that became one of the internet's biggest success stories. In 2013, Bezos also made headlines when he purchased *The Washington Post* in a $250 million deal.

Like Jobs, he started his fledgling company in his garage along with a few employees, but they soon expanded operations into a two-bedroom house. The initial success of the company was meteoric. With no press promotion, Amazon.com sold books across the United States and in 45 foreign countries within 30 days. Within two months, sales reached $20,000 a week, as they grew far faster than Bezos and his startup team had envisioned.

When traditional retailers launched their own e-commerce sites, Amazon not only kept up, but outpaced all competitors, becoming the undisputed e-commerce champion. As they diversified and kept offering more and more via major retail partnerships, Amazon kept right on flourishing with yearly sales that jumped from $510,000 in 1995 to more than $514 billion in 2022.

The Bezos story continued with Kindle, Kindle Fire, and even Blue Origin, a Seattle-based company that has started taking passengers to the edge of space. A respected innovator and business leader, he is in great demand and his Amazon.com continues to move up to 80 percent of books purchased online today!

He is another extraordinary man with all of this to say to anyone who aspires to greatness today:

"When competitors are in the shower in the morning, they're thinking about how they're going to get ahead of one of their top competitors. Here in the shower, we're thinking about how we are going to invent something on behalf of a customer."

"If you never want to be criticized, for goodness' sake don't do anything new."

"One of the only ways to get out of a tight box is to invent your way out."

"Any business plan won't survive its first encounter with reality. The reality will always be different. It will never be the plan."

"All businesses need to be young forever. If your customer base ages with you, you're Woolworth's."

"I very frequently get the question: 'What's going to change in the next 10 years?' And that is a very interesting question; it's a very common one. I almost never get the question: 'What's not going to change in the next 10 years?' And I submit to you that that second question is actually the more important of the two—because you can build a business strategy around the things that are stable in time. ... In our retail business, we know that customers want low prices, and I know that's going to be true 10 years from now…When you have something that you know is true, even over the long term, you can afford to put a lot of energy into it."

"A company shouldn't get addicted to being shiny, because shiny doesn't last."

"Invention requires a long-term willingness to be misunderstood. You do something that you genuinely believe in, that you have conviction about, but for a long period of time, well-meaning people may criticize that effort. When you receive criticism from well-meaning people, it pays to ask, 'Are they right?' And if they are, you need to adapt what they're doing. If they're not right, if you really have conviction that they're not right, you need to have that long-term willingness to be misunderstood. It's a key part of invention."

"You want to look at what other companies are doing. It's very important not to be hermetically sealed. But you don't want to look at it as if, 'OK, we're going to copy that.' You want to look at it and say, 'That's very interesting. What can we be inspired to do as a result of that?' And then put your own unique twist on it."

WARREN BUFFETT, ENTREPRENEUR EXTRAORDINAIRE

Warren Buffett, another who mingles among the richest on the planet, displayed an interest in business and investing at the youngest of ages. One of his first business ventures involved selling chewing gum and weekly magazines. He worked in his grandfather's grocery store, delivered newspapers, sold golf balls and stamps, and detailed cars, among other things. Ever mindful of how to do business, on his first filed tax return in 1944, he took a $35 deduction for the use of his bicycle and watch on his paper route.

Later in life, he went from selling chewing gum to building Berkshire Hathaway, one of the richest enterprises in the world. At points in time, he controlled IBM, General Electric, Coca-Cola, ABC, *The Washington Post*, and many other newspapers and studios.

Buffet is an anomaly who achieves mightily, amasses great wealth and yet decries the fact that one can grow so exorbitantly wealthy in a world where so many exist. So he rejects the materialism and the need for the stuff. Oh sure, he does have the home on the coast of California and recently, as age has dictated, he broke down and bought the long-rejected private plane, but he lives simply and still in the same Omaha home that he purchased for $31,000 in 1957. He has made it clear that he opposes the transfer of great wealth from one generation to the next, so he proposes to give his children just enough and give the rest back to the world.

In the past, he also has complained about the fact that this country enables him to be taxed at 19 percent, while his employees are taxed at 33 percent. The system, he suggests, is unfairly rigged on behalf of the wealthy.

"We have learned to turn out lots of goods and services, but we haven't learned as well how to have everybody share in the bounty. The obligation of a society as prosperous as ours is to figure out how better to share that bounty," said Warren Buffet. To that end, he has pledged to give away the better part of his wealth and he has joined hands with Bill and Melinda Gates in what is now their joint effort to resolve some of the most pressing problems in the world.

In a letter to *Fortune Magazine*'s website in 2010, Buffett remarked:

"My luck was accentuated by my living in a market system that sometimes produces distorted results, though overall it serves our country well... I've worked in an economy that rewards someone who saves the lives of others on a battlefield with a medal, rewards a great teacher with thank-you notes from parents, but rewards those who can detect the mispricing of securities with sums reaching into the billions. In short, fate's distribution of long straws is wildly capricious."

This statement was made as part of a joint proposal with Gates to encourage other wealthy individuals to pool parts of their fortunes for charitable purposes. He is a gifted and extraordinary man with a rich mind, and here is some of his wisdom:

> "Investing in yourself is the best thing you can do. Anything that improves your own talents, nobody can tax it or take it away from you."

> "It's better to hang out with people better than you. Pick out associates whose behavior is better than yours and you'll drift in that direction."

> "You only have to do a very few things right in your life so long as you don't do too many things wrong."

> "Someone's sitting in the shade today, because someone planted a tree a long time ago."

"I don't look to jump over seven-foot bars. I look for one-foot bars that I can step over."

Three Final Arrows

I have only three final arrows in my quiver—some final eye-popping quotes on the nature of success. Consider them this chapter's exclamation point:

"You miss 100 percent of the shots you don't take," said Wayne Gretzky, the NHL Hall of Famer. In other words, he is just urging you to take your shot. And why on earth would you not?

Tom Coughlin, the iconic NFL head coach who led the New York Giants to two Super Bowl victories, said, "Winning is what happens when a commitment, desire, talent, preparation, hard work, and leadership all come together."

And finally, there's the man who may well have become the president of the United States of America, had he lived in 1968: Senator Robert Francis Kennedy, who offered these simple but powerful words: "Only those who dare to fail greatly can ever achieve greatly."

So dare greatly and achieve greatly. In the end, failure is but the province of those who never tried, for only those who try are truly capable of failing.

What Would Charlie Say?

My grandfather never offered a written formula for success—he just lived it through his action, concern for others, and his all-in attitude. Success for him was both reflected and fueled by his own virtues. He demonstrated through his life that success begins on the inside, and that you can learn a great deal from others on your path to achievement. That, in fact, is the theme of this chapter. There is no doubt that with each one of the points made here, he would remind us that we must proceed with humility, faith, courage, independence, responsibility, duty, decency, compassion, goodness, and pride.

5

Building Your Foundation: Time and Tenacity

"There is no elevator for success. You have to take the stairs."
— Zig Ziglar

"Everyone you pass in life has something to teach you."

"You must go the extra mile."
— Charlie

You have taken inventory and identified what you believe to be your purpose and what you know to be your passion. You have done the homework and research as to what it takes to become a player in this field or, at some point, to open a business in this field, just as you have assessed your potential and what credentials you will yet need to acquire. You have identified a mentor or mentors who will hold your hand and guide and advise as you go forward.

You have committed to making this the story that you most want to write about your life, or, as Shell suggests, to make this the suit of clothes that you have determined to wear. You know that this is the song that you want to sing. Your voice now speaks to this, and your physiology, every fiber of you, is tuned into it.

Now it's time to build your foundation—chart the course, and write the plan! It's time to execute and begin the hard work, and that's where the rubber meets the road—with the hard work. What schooling, what classes, what training? Will it be part time or full time? With what job do you attempt to begin? What is the next step, and the step after that? What are the fall back positions or the contingencies?

If there's a point along the way where you expect to venture out on your own, then there is a whole different set of questions that you must confront. On your own, or with partners? And just who might they be?

How do you manage your expenses and budget? What tools, what technology, what software, what social media, what services or goods will you require? What about the selling, advertising, and marketing? What about the public relations and the communications tools, from logos to business cards, to letterhead, to websites, to direct mail? There is no stone that can be left unturned.

Understand that each question often leads to more questions, rather than answers, so dig down deep and go for it. Get the best advice you can and, for goodness' sake, trust yourself.

Also understand that there are no perfect plans, so be prepared to throw one out and start over again–or, at the very least, to adjust and modify the one that you are sticking with. There is only the plan that is destined to work for you, and it is up to you to construct it. With prospective life-altering efforts like this, often, the hardest step is simply determining to take that all-important first step. It is all up to you—your choice and your steps, one after another after another.

It all comes down to building a foundation of time and tenacity.

Taking Advantage of Time

No one manages time. We simply do our level best to take advantage of time. Our goal, revised and revised and revised again, is to use what time we have as best we can.

To think that you can manage time will never actually work, because time to you and me is not the dictionary definition or the "point or period at which things occur." It is rather when stuff actually happens either for or to you.

You live in real time and not in clock time. To you, it is never going to be about the minutes in the hour or the hours in the day, nor is it going to be about the fact that time keeps passing by at the same rate.

To you, time is relative, and it is about the moment the thought that made all the difference came to you. It's about that moment of discovery, or that 10-minute conversation that netted the sponsorship, the deal, the sale, or a new goal. It's about the entire day that can fly by in an instant when you are firing on all cylinders, the day that never seems to end when the engine that is you keeps on misfiring.

When you are happy, time becomes a supersonic jet; when you are sad, time becomes a Model A Ford. Whether or not time is fleeting or agonizing depends on you, because it's not so much about where the handles on the clock are, but rather where your head is, which is where time exists in the first place.

When working, you are always doing one of three things: thinking, having a conversation with someone, or creating (i.e. acting, building, shoveling, forging, writing, studying, etc.). As to the thinking, you do it constantly, but you've got to shut everything else down every once in a while to "just" think. As to the conversing, we're usually good with the talking but we're awfully poor on the listening end. So listen and take on the world. As to the creating, to put it into perspective, even Thomas Edison would come to say, "On the ten-thousandth time, there was light." And it is you who determines just when and how much you will do of each.

There is only your time, and you alone are the master of it. If it matters, it is you who must devote the time that it takes to get the important stuff done.

Those who live in a "there is not enough time" and "this is a wrong time" world are destined neither to achieve nor to succeed.

Time is a tool to be applied and not a limitation. Time invites. It does not demand. It is your friend and not the enemy. You can get control of the power of time by doing the following:

- Think about the day's plan before you begin.
- Keep both a "must-do" and a "to-do" list.
- Do your best to devote a block of time to accomplish the "must-dos," and carry forward whatever "to-dos" don't get completed.
- Schedule time for measuring, assessing, and thinking.
- Keep the appointments you make with yourself.
- Give yourself time to think before key calls and actions.
- Put up the "Do Not Disturb" sign when you must.
- Know that it's never possible to get everything done.
- Before you end your day, consider what really mattered in the day.
- Take that, and build on it for the next day.

Trust this and keep on practicing, no matter how much you come to believe that it doesn't matter. It *does* matter, and you will, over time, become better and better at this.

Focus on improving, tweaking, enhancing, and perfecting how and what you do with your time.

Use time. Take advantage of time. Get into your time.

TIME MANAGEMENT THEORIES

Frederick Taylor's scientific management theories rise to the basic principles of organizational management, which also spawned the principles of time management. The primary goal then and today is increasing your personal productivity. Or, simply and ultimately, getting more done in less time!

It was Frank and Lillian Gilbreth, the subjects of the biographical book-turned-film *Cheaper by the Dozen*, who built upon Taylor's work by conducting time and motion studies that began to focus on the best ways for jobs to be performed. The goal was to maximize and enhance outputs and thus the actual productivity in a given amount of time.

And that, I imagine, is your goal as well.

Back in the day, of course, time management theory was solely the province of white-collar workers. It was all about how many widgets could be produced per hour on an assembly line. So they measured, monitored, standardized, and then trained blue-collar workers accordingly, inevitably producing more and more widgets in less time.

The beat goes on and on today, in that we are all still concerned about using time wisely in order to best advance our own personal goals and dreams.

There are hundreds of variations on the time management theme, but all somehow involve the following. We set goals. We prepare daily action or to-do lists. We prioritize our goals and our "to-dos." We try our best to allocate the amount of time that needs to be devoted to each task.

To do this, we consider and factor in our personal habits and what we know about "our own way of working." We recognize that there will be interruptions, calls, and unexpected delays, so we also schedule times for adjustment and reconsideration. We recognize that those interruptions may require us to devote time to unexpected tasks. So we plan every day for periods of adjustment, periods to deal with the daily surprises, and periods to breathe, to think, and to evaluate.

We must take time out to consider what we have accomplished, and what we need to do better the next day. We should end each day by reprioritizing and planning the next day in light of what we just learned about our planning and ourselves. We keep working at this, hoping that we will, in time, get better at it.

Understand, however, that nothing about this is a perfect science. Frederick Taylor truly believed that we could apply scientific methodology to our ways of working and being. But trust me, there is nothing scientific about managing time.

Of course, many outfits offer time management classes. There also are books on the subject, elaborate day planners that you can buy, and apps for the computer or your cell phone that you can utilize. But it all comes down to how well you apply the guidelines above.

Respect the Work

Another key part of your success foundation is honoring and respecting your work, however menial or seemingly degrading it may be, and even if it's a temporary fix and not a component of your plan. It does not matter, for how you conduct yourself in any job makes a statement about you and who you intend to be. If you intend to succeed and live your best life, cutting corners will not be in your vocabulary.

You must bring your very best to the work at hand, even if it is for the sake of the dignity of the work alone. This is a core principle, for no matter the job, it is to be done as well as humanly possible.

You should impress your superiors with your willingness to go beyond what is required and excel—even if it is for the sake of excellence alone. Strive to put yourself in position for a raise or for a promotion and prospective advancement, even if these are not possible at the moment. Promotions and rewards, I believe, do not come on our time, but they do come. Give your best, and good will follow.

Diligent workers are noticed, appreciated, and celebrated. If not in the position you are in, then certainly in the next stop on your journey to the top.

Inspired by Charlie: Success Tips

- **Do your due diligence:** While you're practicing being productive with your time, remember to be tenacious in doing your "due diligence," or your research on whatever path or strategy you are investigating. By definition, research requires doing the "creative work undertaken on a systematic basis in order to increase your stock of knowledge." Somewhere, someone is always going where no one has ever gone before; and every day, the economy is tweaked, and confidence, in even the most subtle of measurable ways, either rises or falls, and markets move, and things change. And whether for the short or the long term, you must know why.

- **Persevere:** Doing what is worthwhile is rarely easy. To the contrary, it requires a rare dedication and commitment to staying the course when the going gets tough. There will be speed bumps and failings along the way, and sometimes they will come in bunches. This often sends the faint of heart running, but that is not who you are. You must be among the courageous who stay on track despite the setbacks, and who keep bouncing back from them. That's what perseverance is. It is getting back on track after the trains collide. It is going forward even when the fear and doubts set in. It is remaining true to your journey on the way to your best life, no matter what. So, you must keep the faith and never, ever give up. Yes, it is hard, but the prize is monumental. Your purpose realized, your passion nurtured, and your best life lived. So, fight for it and go forward, brick by lonely brick, in the direction of your dreams.

- **Deliver the goods:** No matter where you are on your map or plan—no matter the company, the job, the place, or the time—no matter the external forces—no matter short term or long term—no matter the pay or the prospect for advancement—you must commit yourself to being an always excellent employee. You must make the delivery of excellence on the job a habit. This, also, is part of your foundation for success. Completely applying yourself to the job and task at hand is a core principle. It is the old cut-no-corners, do whatever it takes, come early, stay late, work through lunch, meticulously deliver principle.

- **Exceed all expectations:** Whether you are an entry-level employee, rising in a better job, or where you want to be in your own business, you must go the extra mile every single day. You must make "come early, stay late, skip that lunch, do more, and work harder" a mantra and a habit. Not just one day, but day after day. Yes, you must breathe and take the time needed to love and care and serve and play and worship, but when at work and on task, you must give your best always. The motto is, "I will be exceptional and I will exceed all expectations." The mantra is, "If you are always trying to be normal, you'll never know just how amazing you can be." Be extraordinary. Be amazing.

- **Follow through:** Always do what you say that you are going to do. If that means calling someone at 3 p.m. tomorrow, within the next 24 hours, or next month, do it. Oddly enough, this will impress the client because most people fail to follow up as they intend to. They are sloppy, something that you are not going to be. If you say it, remember it and make it happen. If you offer something to someone, if you say you'll eat the costs of the copying or the mailing or UPS or FedEx, if you quote a price—write it down, make a note of it, and be diligent in following through.

There's No Shame in Punting and Switching Gears

Also consider this: You were given free will, so you are forever free to change your mind and move in another direction. Accordingly, if your plan goes bust due to forces beyond your control, then tear it up, throw it away, and construct a new one. So too is it with failure, for when you fall or fail, like we all do, the trick is to immediately pick yourself back up, dust yourself off, and try again.

So what? You lose some time and you're rattled and unsteady for a time. Know that all such negativity will wash away when you get back on solid ground and set off in the direction of your real purpose.

Again, I remind you of the profound words of one of the bravest men in history, the World War II prime minister of England, Winston Churchill, who said, "Success is stumbling from failure to failure with no loss of enthusiasm." I love that. Your soul and your spirit must be invested in whatever you are pursuing. If the spirit is not in it, the heart and mind will never follow.

One door shuts and another opens. Chin up and eyes straight, just walk on through and start writing your story.

Polishing Your Personal Qualities

For any prospective client, referral or chance inquiry, there can be no, "Well, it was just another phone call"—no *que sera, sera*—no complaints about their attitude—no "we didn't need them anyway." Everyone must be made to feel special. Sure, we all have tough days and bad moments, but when you pick up that phone, or when someone walks into your office, either your employee or you had better be on. You are, after all, about to go on stage, and the audience expects nothing less than the very best that you have to give.

It is equally important to be confident and informative. And if it is left to staff, because you are out, then they must convey the fact that you indeed will know and that you will get back to them in a minimal number of hours. They must be point certain about this, so you must be point certain with them. The amount of prospective business lost in this exchange is astounding, business that would not be lost if they only received that return phone call in a matter of hours.

Never guess or exaggerate. Be honest at all times, and if you don't have the answer, assure them that you will get it and get back to them with it by a specific time in the immediate future (never more than 24 hours). Don't ever give an answer that you're not sure of. That's one absolute death knell to the growth-success formula.

Assuring the Quality of Your Product or Service

Now, it goes without saying that it is still very important to make sure that your product or service is of the highest quality, and that your price point is marketplace competitive—because, unfortunately, no matter how great they may feel about you, no one ever is looking to pay any more than they have to. Now, don't get me wrong, I am a big believer in value added. The very best and most legendary providers in a region can price higher and get away with it, and people will and do pay more when they are confident that someone can "deliver the goods" without any setbacks or glitches.

But stray too far from the pack and you will likely be punished by not getting the business. As for me, I deliver the goods as an expert and confidently feel that I am one of the best in the mortgage industry.

Through great effort, I have established a value-added reputation, but I still make sure the mortgage rates and fees being offered are competitive, if not better than the marketplace. The clients get my expertise along with exceptional service throughout the entire loan process, at no additional cost. That's truly value-added.

Why should they pay me more, because I have delivered for others in the past or because I'm better at doing what I should be doing for them in the first place? While I could likely get away with a value-added price point at this juncture, I look upon going there as professional arrogance where ego and greed get in the way of who one is.

Don't Run

Renowned American photographer Diane Arbus said, "Regardless of how you feel inside, always try to look like a winner." So it is with your clients. Even when a relationship is not working out as expected, do not abruptly drop a job and run away. Take your leave of the client professionally and via mutual agreement. Even when you exit, do it like a winner! This appears to be a secret, given that so many easily pull the plug on one client as they rush off to be with another. They suffer under the delusion that being busy impresses, when the fact is that it annoys and even angers.

Standing Out by Going the Extra Mile

Go to conventions or events that apply to your industry. Attend seminars, converse with everyone, speak to the instructors, ask questions, and absorb as much information as you possibly can. Make yourself known through as many events as possible.

Eventually, you want to work your way in to speak or instruct at these conferences. After all, to truly stand out, you must be an expert in your industry. Walk the walk and talk the talk. Be greater. Be the greatest. Be the expert who can talk your industry's language. I promise that opportunities and business will come from it.

Learning from Others

Listen to your mentor or mentors. Talk to those who did it before you. Listen with both ears and learn from those who fought in the trenches long before the advance of all the modern bells and whistles. There's nothing better than going to the living sources who have stories to tell and wisdom to share. They might not be on top of the latest news, but they'll surely inspire you.

Listening, as I noted earlier, is a lost art. We may think we are listening, but we rarely hear. Working on that alone will go a long way.

Finding Your Own Tech Wizard

Today, it is technology that must define and express that purpose and passion of yours. Technology will also enable you to present yourself as the best, so that's part of your foundation. In the corporate world, the likelihood is that your employer will have the technological wizards on board to assist you and guide you in this quest. But if you're going down your own road, you must utilize or discover the technological wizard inside you or tap the assistance and guidance of the wizards for hire who are always lurking within striking distance.

Technology and enterprise are married today, and the simple, understated truth is that your ability to utilize technological advances or not can literally make or break your success.

I have no intention of overplaying my hand here, for I am not now nor will I ever be the tech guy, but I do know enough to know what I need and what the limits of the possible are. I do what I can, I get help when needed, and I have been smart enough to make sure the branch staff has their own fair share of technological savvy.

This is how I can send out semi-monthly informational newsletters with useful information for current and prospective clients.

If any of that information brings them to my website, or if they email me a question, all well and good! I do hope they will remember to call upon me if the need arises, but these emails definitely help to keep my name in front of them. I do not overtly sell, but rather *support*. The point is that I utilize technology to communicate with the thousands of contacts in my database who are able to benefit from my services or refer me to their contacts. In Chapter 6, "Building and Managing Your Network," I provide more detail on these newsletters, and how you can design your own for maximum impact.

Remember That Communication Is Everything

Technology allows for improved response times. The emails, the texts, the calls—I celebrate the all of it. I respond in the moment as a demonstration of respect. If further research is needed, I respond immediately, and then follow up as quickly as humanly possible. The fast response impresses them and makes them realize that they are dealing with someone who cares.

In the nitty-gritty of communication lie the keys to anyone's success.

Another tech secret of mine has to do with putting people on hold. In most offices, when on hold you typically are met by either music or by silence. I actually take advantage of the time to enhance my marketing efforts by having a professional voice explain the services we offer while soft music is playing in the background.

As to the equipment, know that you don't have to buy the most expensive or the top of the line. Just be sure that the functionality is there—and these days you can do almost anything from a mobile phone! Most importantly, however, and where you do want the best, is in your Wi-Fi and internet service. You do not want to be slowed down.

If communication is everything (and it is), and if you are efficiently utilizing technology to drive that communication (as you should), you don't ever want it to break down because connections get lost or because the service, like the turtle, is moving like molasses in soft soap.

Real time, after all, means *fast*.

A last word on technology: When in doubt, get help. It is always available.

Taking the Necessary Risks

To live is always an adventure, so take the mighty risks that truly living demands. You must be willing to risk and dare if you are ever to maximize success or to live your best life. It takes courage to say no to the status quo and commit to building an entirely different life, and it is largely a lack of courage that precludes so many from reaching out for their best life.

Many people stay safe in the harbor and accept what comes rather than venture out onto the high seas to explore what may be. Consider the words of John A. Shedd, an America author and professor: "A ship in harbor is safe, but that is not what ships are built for." So dare to be you, dare to live your purpose and passion, dare to make your dreams come true, and dare to both envision and then live your best life.

Yes, I already have quoted our old friend, Henry David Thoreau and his plea to you to build your "castles in the air" and then put in the "foundations." He is talking about your life— one destined to know happiness, love, service, and goodness! A full and complete life!

What Would Charlie Say?

Charlie was all about using time wisely and staying tenacious in order to build a strong foundation for success. He took his time to listen to everyone growing up, then learned and acted upon his acquired knowledge. "Everyone you pass in life has something to teach you," he said. Even though he was in many ways a simple man, by listening to the brokers and investment bankers at Zeta Psi, he was able to find success in investing while becoming a confidant to his era's top movers and shakers. He also said, "It's not your wages that give you a good life. It is your wisdom." He knew that no matter what the job, you needed to respect the work, give it your all, and grab the brass ring.

6

Building and Managing Your Network

"In order to have friends, you must be one."
— Elbert Hubbard

"No one ever does it alone."
— Charlie

I simply love networking, because I love meeting new people. I enjoy the networking dance, and the opportunity, expectations, chances, and wonder that come with it. Maybe you'll meet a person with whom you can do business, or maybe you'll meet someone who is destined to become a new friend. Maybe you'll even meet someone with whom you will form an alliance. And, just maybe, that person will become your business partner in the future.

I played sports, and I love everything from soccer to football to baseball. A networking event is like a sport. Networking is a game that counts. It's real life, and it has a playing field that metaphorically enables me to score all of the runs and make all of the touchdowns, and help others score also. Yes, it not only counts, but I get to be an active participant in my own success as well as in the success of others.

All it takes is making a few contacts or even one lasting connection. With networking, there are no limits. There are just limitless possibilities.

Learn From Everyone

Each person you encounter knows more about something than you do. So, listen to everyone, and learn always. In the most nondescript and humblest of places, there is always a teacher waiting for you.

Charlie, as you already know, was absolutely adamant about this. "Every person on the street has something to teach you," he always said. To live your best life demands that you be a lifelong learner who extracts new knowledge and information from all those you encounter.

Build Relationships to Build Your Best Life

Building relationships, especially lasting relationships, is essential to any business or venture. No matter what path you choose to go down in life, you will never stop working on building relationships. As Charlie always told me, "It's not what you know, but who you know, that counts most." You can supercharge this strategy by serving charitable, civic, community, and business service organizations, through which even more relationships evolve.

When you meet someone, what you always take away are those "first blush" senses and feelings as to whether or not you might build a friendship or professional relationship with them. You make an assessment of their trust, ability, smarts, and other important qualities. However, you cannot be sure, and you will not be sure until you get to know them—if you get to know them. Still, you're generally more right than wrong about those first blush impressions. So, all you can do is trust yourself and look to follow up with those you meet who, for whatever reason, made your A-list.

While you are encountering and assessing people who may be able to help you, also think about others in your business and personal life, and look out for them. If you have an idea, referral, or prospective opportunity for them, make the connection, pass it along, and help them to succeed. Believe me, if you do this as routinely as you brush your teeth or grab that morning cup of coffee, you will build a mighty network of friends, and the business and good karma will come back to you in spades. I know, with absolute certainty, that doing good and being a positive force for others makes an incredible difference and attracts people to you like a magnet.

I regularly look at ways to develop new relationships, because therein lies the best generator of new business. Business development never takes a day off. Existing relationships maintain and sustain, but the new relationships are just as important. A great way to build your network is by connecting with the colleagues and clients of people in your existing database that already know you and, more importantly, already refer business to you. This is truly "the secret" to building an incredibly successful referral-based business.

On another note, since we spend more time working with our colleagues, referral partners, and clients than we get to spend with our own family and friends, it is very important to surround yourself with good people who you enjoy being with. These people will also play a major part helping you advance in your field and grow as a person. And, as I have said many times, make sure that you also help others advance as individuals and in their careers. The positive energy of giving is very powerful. Be a giver and you will see incredible things happen.

One More Take on Your Mentors

I'm going to digress for a bit to emphasize the fact that the act of securing a mentor or mentors who can advise, guide, and help you shape your plan is so very critical. After all, there is no course in school on how to script a life's plan.

Let's be honest: You might have a clue as to what you know your avocation to be, and what your purpose might be, but even the best of us need help and guidance in charting a course and finding the best way to get there. If you are misfiring from the get go, all the action in the world won't make any difference and, lest we forget, your attitude is likely to wind up in some toilet somewhere.

Look to the field or industry that you have set your sights on, identify leaders in that field, and ask a select few for their help. Look to teachers, professors, "big brothers," community leaders, chambers of commerce, and people you respect who can help you. Do a Google search and reach out to mentoring organizations in your area as well. They are cropping up everywhere and they are available to you. For no matter how bright and self-starting and good you are, the helping hand of seasoned, experienced pros lightens the load and introduces you to ideas and possibilities that you may never have even considered.

Interestingly, I received a notice inviting me to a National Mentoring Conference at the University of New Mexico. This event was attended by educators on all levels, researchers, community leaders, administrators, non-profit directors, government officials, and professionals in diverse industries, all of whom either already were mentors or prospective mentors—increasingly known as "developmental leaders." Their marketing material focused on the concept of forging developmental relationships, be they mentoring, coaching, or leading. The conference theme was "A *Quest for Leadership Excellence & Innovation*," and the keynote speaker presented a speech entitled, "*The Leadership Journey: Transformative Leaps for Humankind.*"

Similarly, workshop topic headings included the following:

- Building on the knowledge base of existing literature in the field of developmental relationships.

- Demonstrating the effectiveness of existing mentoring programs.

- Proposing a methodology or evaluation model for developmental relationships.

- Suggesting new ideas and best practices for successful mentoring and developmental relationships.

- Proposals that include participants of different nationalities, different levels of experience, and from different institutional and organization types.

I share this to hammer away at the fact that there are legions of folks out there who are interested in your ability to garner a mentor, and develop that one special relationship that will bring the best out of you. Somewhere in the midst of their *Transformative Leaps for Humankind*, you are being singled out.

You are the target. You are the possibility and the promise that they are after. Yes, out there, in New Mexico, these unknown professors and academics are thinking about you, but it is you who must do your own angling, opting, researching, planning, and leaping.

Mastering the Art of Networking

Through networking, you cultivate productive relationships for employment, business, or enterprise. I like to describe it as net working, with a hard emphasis on the working part. It takes a lot of time, energy, sacrifice, commitment, and dedication to build the kind of relationships that both work and last. Networking, in effect, is a portal to or a tool via which to develop new relationships.

Networking can take place in multiple ways, from ongoing connections and sharing through LinkedIn, Clubhouse (an audio app with chat rooms), Facebook, and other popular social media platforms, to perhaps the strongest networking medium of all—the traditional in-person event, whether a networking breakfast, conference, or trade show. From event to event, every single networking opportunity is rich with promise and unbridled possibility. By definition, networking is "the exchange of information or services among individuals, groups, or institutions; the cultivation of formative and productive relationships for employment or business."

Networking events, whether traditional or supported by digital platforms, often are sponsored by chambers of commerce, professional associations, and even civic and community organizations. They are specifically designed to bring people together in order to advance their business and professional purposes. People attend with the absolute intention of connecting with others with whom they might exchange reciprocal leads in the hope of generating either business or interest in their work. You must remember that the most important aspect about networking is that it is a two-way street. You cannot be there for your own self-interest only, or people will see right through you.

To get something, you must be willing to give something in return.

MAKING A PRODUCTIVE CONNECTION

If you attended an event, an interactive seminar, or a virtual gathering on Clubhouse and left feeling like you met someone who might fit into that inner circle of people with whom you both receive and refer business, then that is just great. You did everything right! Hopefully, you found a valuable future colleague, supplier or customer who could become part of your inner circle, and with whom you have the reasonable expectation of doing business.

When you meet someone like this, never be afraid to ask if they already have someone in your field with whom they exchange business referrals. If they say no, you are all set and good to go; if they say yes, then dig a little deeper. Maybe they'll say that they do have someone, but that it's not exclusive, and they would still be happy to recommend you as well. Then, it's a judgement call.

Sometimes, you may actually get real lucky and meet someone who could actually use your services and you walk away with a warm lead and a potential client.

What has opened up those new vistas for me is simply this: For those who I feel have something special to offer (and believe me, you'll know this in a matter of minutes) I set up a follow-up breakfast or lunch meeting on the spot. I respectfully and courteously pin them down and say that we need to learn more about each other's businesses, and to better explore just how we might be able to help one another.

The thing that I find most satisfying about networking can only happen after you have built a good reputation and truly networked with a lot of people. It is as simple as walking over to someone you know well, or who is a client, and then being introduced to the person or people they happen to be speaking with as "Marc Demetriou, the best mortgage guy I know."

Wow—how can I then not go to every networking event possible? And, as soon as some kind friend says something like that, I humbly say, "Thank you very much for that kind introduction, one that prompts me to give you all my card now as I ask you to tell me a bit about what you do." Yes, they invariably accept it happily. But, of course, don't ever forget to ask for theirs as well in order to put them into your database or network. In it, you record all the business basics, along with any significant personal notes or assessments about them that struck you.

Remember, knowing something about their spouse, children, interests, favorite place, etc. is invaluable, because it allows you to relate and to be appropriately personal with them in the future.

STRATEGIC ALLIANCES

Strategic alliances can be extremely important to you, and are reserved for the very special people who you get to know very well over the course of a number of follow-up meetings. The purpose of the strategic alliance is for both parties to commit to sending business to each other. Be sure to keep a list of your strategic alliance partners' contact information on your phone, as well as in a printed list on your desk or taped to your monitor.

This will serve as a reminder for you to always think about the fortunate members in your strategic alliances, and it almost guarantees that you will be sending business their way regularly. Believe me, if they understand how this works, and if they are true, they will keep you in mind and send business your way as well.

You should catch up with your strategic partners regularly, not to compare lead counts, but simply to stay in tune and to advise one another of any important updates or new products that will help you better promote each other. If 12 months pass, and you have sent five leads to one member, while that person has sent none, it's definitely time for a meeting or reckoning to assess why and whether or not it makes sense to hold on to their partnership.

This is not just about being on the receiving end. With a strategic alliance, it is vital to have the right partners because you do have good leads and value to offer, and some reciprocation is only fair. Not one for one, necessarily, but you must know that there is, at least, active consideration and concern on their part.

The Rules of Networking

Whether it is a chamber of commerce, association, or other business group, there are some very simple rules to follow when it comes to networking. These can differ, depending on whether you are at a local town sporting event, a reception for some charity, a party, a luncheon with a prominent speaker, or at a networking event.

At all events associated with your personal life and the life of your family, any attempt to market yourself must be low key. I like to say that any marketing here requires going in through the proverbial "back door," since the "front door" is always closed in such settings—and, even then, only when and if a reasonable opportunity arises.

You pitch only when and if someone says something that opens that back door up for you. Think covertly and be creative. For instance, plant the seeds of a related conversation that might evolve in the direction of your expertise. I always bring up mortgage rates or something about the housing market, and eventually I tell them what to do. Most of the time, it leads to them asking me questions related to their mortgage, or something they are planning to do related to housing.

At non-family events, you are free to be upfront and to sell yourself. But there is a primary and formative issue to always keep in mind: Everyone is there for the same reason, and you must be respectful of that. If you are solely focused on your own self-interests, people will smoke you out and see right through you.

At in-person events, the people who walk around saying hello and handing out their business card within the first five seconds of meeting someone are, most certainly, very poor networkers. My rule is to always be for the other first. Before they learn anything about me, I want to know about them, and I want to share a few positive thoughts or suggestions with them.

Believe me, within the first minute of meeting, people will get a feel for whether or not they like you, are interested in what you have to say, or believe that you might be someone whom they can trust. The greatest compliment is being told by someone who you just met that they feel comfortable talking with you and already sense that they can trust you. It is a gift to have won someone's trust, because that is the epicenter of every personal, professional, and business relationship.

Without trust, you stand still—you go nowhere.

In short, networking is truly the province of those who are sincere, honest, caring, thoughtful and honorable. The fakers just won't get very far. Oh, they might succeed at the short game for a while, but they will never go long.

Inspired by Charlie: Success Tips

- Act to forge relationships: My grandfather Charlie, more than anyone in my life, taught me that building a relationship can be a pleasure—an absolutely clear and simple joy—but it demands that you take concerted action. It may even include a measure of work on your part. When you meet someone, you should, within a 24-hour period, send a short follow-up email that says how good it was to connect. Offer encouragement and ask how you can help them. Briefly remind them of what you do, and that you hope they will think of you when in need of your service or simply in need of information about the same. Additionally, if you want to meet a particular person, ask to meet for coffee or breakfast to get to know each other better.

- Join, join, join: Get your world to know that you exist and be loud about it. Join every business and professional association that you can and become involved. Volunteer and contribute—be a giver and work it. Don't lay back and wait for the chamber or the association to happen to you, but rather happen to it. Here you establish reputation and here you build relationships and develop networks and engage people and institutions who are going to help you fulfill your dreams. Aim to be a leader and not a follower. Never forget that you give and you receive, and then you ascend. In his own way, Charlie did all of this. He was a master networker.

Never Stop Building Your Network

The more people you know, the more successful you can and will become. Again, as Charlie and many others always have said, "It's not what you know; it's *who* you know" is so true. You need your schooling and your degrees, but being a "people person" and someone who is very "networked" will allow you to achieve great success. You want as many people as possible to always be thinking about you when a business opportunity arises.

If you exude passion, enthusiasm, compassion, and expertise in your field, along with a commitment to excellence, you will not be forgotten. Be an active member in your local chamber of commerce, town boards, industry associations, and charitable organizations. If you're so inclined and qualified, it's also beneficial from a networking perspective to coach town sports. The bottom line: always continue to nurture your existing contacts, along with the people they know.

Telling the World

Overall, networking is for making lasting connections and becoming well known. It is about building both short-term and long-term business relationships. It is about telling the world that you are an honorable and good person, and an expert in your field who can be trusted to deliver. It is about convincing those you meet that you will do well by their clients. It is about branding yourself as the go-to guy or gal. It is about in-your-face, personal, close and upfront marketing—for me, the most satisfying kind. It is tangible, real, and immediate.

It is about telling the world that you are the expert who can deliver the goods.

Everyone could use a great attorney, accountant, realtor, mortgage expert, business banker, insurance agent, financial planner, electrician, contractor, etc. to refer business to. Your purpose is to be so impressive that you make everyone's list. Ultimately, I literally look upon everyone as a prospective client either now or in the future. Unrealistic, maybe, but that's what I aspire to.

Why shouldn't everyone be referring business to me? Don't think for a moment that this is about ego. It's about service and truly knowing that I go above and beyond each and every time. I am wired to do anything and everything to deliver greater value. Sure, my match may well be out there, but I know, in my head and heart, that I'm as good as it gets.

I'll move mountains for my clients before ever disappointing them. You, of course, must aspire to do the same. If you truly want to succeed, simply determine to be the best and you cannot miss your mark. It is in you and up to you.

Managing Your Contacts

It is important to keep and manage your collection of contacts so that you can put them to use for maximum success. Fortunately, there are many contact management apps out there—most with mobile versions that sinc with your PC—which are low-cost and pretty easy to use! These include Google Contacts, Contact+, Insightly, HubSpot (free!) and many others.

Your growing list certainly should include every prospect and client. You need to keep this information up-to-date, and take the time to enter new information on a timely basis. Also, it is very important to put them into categories by industry so that you can send specific information or updates that will relate to them. They will appreciate the information.

I usually like to send my entire contacts list, which is thousands of people, some important information about twice a month. It might be about economic indicators, the housing market, legal issues, interest rates, credit report information or anything important that people might appreciate knowing related to real estate or finance.

What you want to offer them can never be overt advertising, but rather timely and helpful information that just happens to come with your face, name and company name and/or logo attached to it—a service, if you will, that is associated with you. I usually begin with an inspirational quote that is meant to both move and impact. Constant Contact, which let's you integrate imagery and a message in each mailing, has become the market-dominant app for this, and it available for as low as $9.99 per month. MailChimp also is popular, and it absolutely free at its basic service level!

Whichever app you use to send your messages, remember that the subject line is very important, because it determines whether or not someone opens the email to begin with. In my business, these two simple points of contact each month have generated so much business for me that it shocks me that everybody else isn't doing it. It is a vital component in enhancing reputation and becoming better known for what you do, as well as staying top-of-mind when the need arises.

This is all very easy to do and incredibly productive.

I also advise sending your emails out during the middle of the week and toward the middle of the day. Early in the week, people are too busy to read extra emails, and toward the end of the week, people are focusing on winding down for the weekend. I also like to send them in the middle of the week because I usually get a good amount of responses, and I want to get back to those people by Thursday or Friday at the absolute latest. In fact, if I can't get back to them by the end of the day on Wednesday, I send them a personal email letting them know that I will respond in more depth by Thursday or Friday. If there happens to be an immediate need for my services, this will generally keep them from going somewhere else, but if they advise me that it can't wait, they become a top priority.

I have already written about the passion that I have for responding to any communications almost instantly. You already know how crazy and over the top I am about this. People in my network are often impressed when I respond to them so quickly.

I love doing that! When you impress, you enhance your reputation, and a great reputation equals growth and success. After all, "If you build it, they will come."

Your Social Media

A professional presence on social media—whether LinkedIn, Instagram, Twitter, Facebook or other platforms—can be an effective, low-cost way to raise your visibility and attract new business. It's marketing, and the best way to take advantage of it is to create attractive account pages with your name, logo, and message front and center. Then, you want to post new content to these platforms often—at least three times per week. (According to multiple surveys, You will get the most consistent engagement on Tuesdays through Thursdays from 9 a.m. to 3 p.m. The worst day is Sunday.) Make sure what you post contains valuable information that others may want to share.

However, you can't just post and expect followers, let alone leads, suddenly appear. You need to build your social media audience through your existing contacts and other tools.

To begin, make sure your social media links are in every one of your regular emails and newsletters, along with a blurb that encourages readers to follow you for additional, useful information as it becomes available. This will help your business gain more followers, which in turn, will help your social marketing campaigns better perform. You can also use third-party services to further build your followers. You should be aiming for thousands of followers! Just remember, keep your focus on your or your company's professional skills and offerings.

Going forward, incorporate your email marketing strategy with your social media marketing strategy. That way, you can attract new customers while building and expanding your current networking relationships!

Final Thoughts

There is no getting away from the fact that being a good networker turns on the confidence and the faith that you have in yourself. It turns on the simple ability to relate to people on their terms and not yours. It turns on knowing all that you could ever possibly need to know about your product, service, art or cause. It turns on your belief in yourself and in knowing that you truly have something of value to offer. Be the best, be yourself, be open and caring, and this tremendous resource will open up doors and unimagined new vistas for you.

What Would Charlie Say?

"No one ever does it alone." That's what Charlie said. And he truly lived that. He was all about networking, whether it was schmoozing with the influential up-and-comers from Yale at the Zeta Psi fraternity house, the celebrities at the West Side Tennis Club, or the Wall Street guys at the Downtown Angler's Club. Charlie didn't have their level of pedigree or formal education, but he listened, worked hard for them, gave back in spades, and earned their valuable trust, becoming a confidant to several of America's leaders in business and entertainment. Charlie intuitively knew to ally, trust, and build with others. He learned from everyone willing to offer knowledge or assistance. It all contributed to his success, as it will to yours.

7

Off and Running

"Twenty years from now you will be more disappointed by the things that you didn't do than by the ones you did do. So throw off the bowlines. Sail away from the safe harbor. Catch the trade winds in your sails. Explore. Dream. Discover."
— Mark Twain, Author

"Be thankful for what you have."
"There are no limits and no ends."
"Believe in yourself always."
"Be joyful."
— Charlie

In this work I have given you my heart, as well as my best thoughts about the tools for achievement and success inspired by my grandfather, Haralambos Georgiou "Charlie" Pistis. These tools have helped me achieve my own dream, and now it is time for them to work for you.

There will always be more to say, more to quote, and more to suggest, but my primary principles are:

- ❦ Explore yourself. Be a "Columbus" to the hidden worlds within.

- ❦ Identify your unique purpose and passion.

- Identify mentors or guides who will be there to advise you.

- Develop an action plan that will lead you to the position and to the place that you imagine.

- Proceed to execute your plan.

- Maintain a positive, upbeat, determined attitude always.

- Form great habits (everything from hygiene, to appearance, to punctuality, to returning messages and inquiries as quickly as humanly possible).

- Arrive early, skip lunch, stay late and volunteer—aim to give more to every class, every workshop, every job and every demeaning or painstaking task.

- Be the very best that you can be at whatever you are doing.

- Never stop learning.

- Become the expert in your field.

- Network and build new relationships always.

- Give back to others in service along the way.

- Nurture your goodness and grace.

- Make a difference not only in your field, but also in your community.

- Find the joy in it all, and never stop smelling the roses along the way.

- Climb to your particular mountaintop, and never stop advancing.

While what I write applies to all, I can't help but envision you—a high school or college student, a recent graduate starting your first job, or a young businessperson early in your career—you "dreamers of dreams" who may not have even begun your journey. I beg you to live in the light of a purpose and a passion, with a plan and goals that magnificently inspire you!

As purpose and passion inspire, so will you be inspired. Even when the final bugle summons you, that inspiration will still be calling you to do more. That's because there always is more.

Inspired by Charlie: The FORMIDABLE Five Success Tips

Of all of the wisdom that Charlie gave to me through the way he lived his life, the wonderful advice that I have boiled down and adapted to fuel my own success, there are five essentials:

1. **Attitude is everything:** You must always remain positive and refuse to let despair into your life. Your disposition and the way you carry yourself have everything to do with just how you advance in your own story. One of the greatest weapons that you possess is your smile. It disarms, it opens doors, it invites, and it encourages, so wear yours always. Stay upbeat and display your commitment to giving your very best always and delivering the goods. Be open about your determination to exceed expectations. When gentleness is warranted, be gentle. When strength is needed, be strong. When compassion is warranted, be compassionate. Be exactly what a good human being should be. Be a believer, a force, a friend. Wear the fact that you are a winner.

2. **Build relationships to create your best life:** Serve charitable, civic, community, and business service organizations. You'll be repaid not only in the knowledge that you're doing good works, but in the valuable relationships you build. Think about others in your business and personal life, and look out for them. If you have an idea, referral, or prospective opportunity for them, make the connection

and pass it along. If you do this as routinely as you brush your teeth or grab that morning cup of coffee, you will have built a mighty network of friends and the business and good karma will come back to you in spades.

3. **Manage your contacts effectively:** You must have a program or service to collect and store the contact information of every single person you know and meet, including every prospect, client, and strategic partner. You need to keep this information up-to-date, so update it on a timely basis. When you meet someone new, you should email them within 24 hours, letting them know that you were pleased to meet them, and that you are hopeful that you will be able to work together and serve each other.

4. **Manage your time effectively:** This is something that you never stop working on. You must determine just how much time to devote to communications, to marketing, to sales, to development, to staff, to finance, and to all the rest. Only you know exactly what you have to do. Break it down into all of its parts, prioritize, and devote the time required to each component or task. It is always a question of that which matters most in the moment. Bob and weave accordingly, but never ignore the essentials.

5. **Develop speaking skills:** Learning to speak, make professional presentations, and effectively market yourself matters a great deal, because it sets you apart and automatically places you on a higher level. Stepping up to be a panelist at workshops, and stepping further still to confront full audiences, distinguishes you. Naturally, it is very important that you be able to converse with anyone about what you

do and how you do it. You should have your 30-second commercial about your skills burned into your brain, and you should be certain that it comes off as very informative, to the point, and from the heart.

How Hard Will You Run?

It amazes me when I stop and think of all of the divergent references that I have utilized in this book, so many of them surprisingly coming from children's authors and fantasies. Here is one more from Lewis Carroll's classic, *Alice in Wonderland*: "You have to run as fast as you can to stay where you are and you have to run twice as fast if you want to get anywhere."

Isn't that the truth! And, while it is the ready byproduct of simple common sense, isn't it also, just maybe, the most important secret of all? Charlie knew it. He dared to dream, and knew in his heart that as long as one had faith enough to risk, dare, and go boldly into the unknown, success would follow.

This means that when working toward your goals, you have to hit the ground running and never look back. Yes, it is a marathon and not a sprint, and yes, there is no elevator, and you have to climb the stairs. Reaching your goals is all about will. If you are willing to go all out to run the race, and if you are inspired every day to advance, you cannot fail—you will not fail—and you will come to live the life that you imagine.

But you have got to want it and you have got to want it badly.

This doesn't mean that you are destined to do nothing but work and run yourself ragged and out of your mind, but it does mean that you have to wake up every day inspired, determined, and committed to giving that day and each moment in it your level best.

Conjuring Mr. Rogers

Mr. Rogers was an ordained Christian minister who found his flock and life's calling in a TV show about a neighborhood. Yes, Fred Rogers, like Lewis Carroll and Dr. Seuss, talked to children, but when you cut through it all, he was ultimately talking to them about appreciating and developing the habits that would enable them to live fulfilling and successful lives.

The quote from our beloved Mr. Rogers is this:

"I think appreciation is a holy thing, that when we look for what's best in a person we happen to be with in that moment, we're doing what God does all the time. So in loving and appreciating our neighbor, we're participating in something sacred."

What a profound thought and extraordinary reminder to us all.

As you advance, remember that real success—a best life kind of success—can never be just about you. Ultimately, you get what you give in life, and the goodness and grace that you "sacredly" extend to others will be returned to you in abundance.

The mind turns to stories like those of Ebenezer Scrooge of *A Christmas Carol* and Mr. Potter of *It's a Wonderful Life*, our classic misers, or even Gordon Gekko of Wall Street, whose great greed consumed him. The point is so simple and so clear: Real success is never and can never be just about the money. It has to be about goodness, as I have said often in these pages. It doesn't hurt to hammer it home one last time, because you deserve the whole package: a happy family, love, community, goodness, grace, enough money to live in peace, and the wherewithal to contribute of your time, money, and talent to whomever may need it, or whatever charity may be fortunate to have your involvement. Do all of these things, and you will have a life one can only dream of.

Whatever You Are, Be a Good One

I began this journey by quoting President Abraham Lincoln, the man who led America through its great Civil War and his very simple but revealing line, "Every man is proud of what he does well; and no man is proud of what he does not do well." Nothing clearer about that which we all ought to be in life. Whatever it is that you choose to be or to do in life, be good and do it well. Give it your best—every minute, every hour, every day, every year.

In a multitude of ways, I have hammered away at the primary premise of all of this—that you make the decision as to whether you achieve your dreams or not, and just what kind of success yours will be. It is absolutely a choice and a decision that you alone make. You choose, you determine, you decide. Without the will and the determination, it cannot be.

A best life is a blessed life. It is being in that place where you have the great fortune of realizing that there is in your "having been," an "ever will be."

Remember, also, Lincoln's many other quotes of inspiration, which included, "Give me six hours to chop down a tree and I will spend the first four sharpening the axe," "I am a slow walker, but I never walk back," and "If you want to succeed, keep believing in yourself even when nobody else does."

In just these four quotes, the savior of our country and the liberator of the slaves spoke to the importance of truly running the race and of going forward without looking back, while at the same time staying true and keeping faith with yourself and also, and finally, of recognizing that four-fifths of the game is in the preparation.

You're Responsible for Your Own Success

Early on in this book, I suggested that just as you are given life, you also are invited into its fullness both spiritually and practically, and it will not quit on you nor let you down unless you quit on yourself and let yourself down. In fact, as Maya Angelou always preached, you were not born to fit in, but rather to stand out. She wrote, "If you are always trying to be normal, you'll never know how amazing you can be."

You are the sole guarantor in your life. As it has so often been said, "You are the master of your destiny. You are the captain of your soul." You and you alone turn the wheel as you sail the ship that is your life. Success is driven by what is already inside of you, patiently waiting to be transformed or activated. My commitment to you in writing this was to help you get to a place where you maximize your potential and succeed.

"So be sure when you step," wrote Dr. Seuss. "Step with care and great tact. And remember that life's a great balancing act. And will you succeed? Yes! You will, indeed! 98 and ¾ percent guaranteed!"

I learned that life lesson about the opportunity that is always lurking early on. You must first open your eyes in order to see it, and then you must tap the ambition lurking inside you that it takes to pursue it. Then, you must do it. Success is high energy, hard work, and full speed ahead, all of the time.

"Who Am I?"

Earlier in this book, I wrote about that most important simple question. It's the old cry of Thoreau for all of us, to "be a Columbus to whole new continents and worlds within you, opening new channels, not of trade, but of thought." You may think of it as self-exploration, self-examination, or even painful personal probing. Who am I? What do I believe? What do I want out of life? What do I most want to contribute? What am I destined to become? Why, what, when, how, if? There are so many questions, but ultimately there is only one true and perfect answer.

The answers are yours and yours alone to determine, and whatever you determine becomes the lightning rod for your life's adventure and journey.

Simply put, the journey on the road to success and a best life begins only when you have truly confronted and met your own purpose and passion, and only when you have discovered what makes your heart sing.

Charlie said, "I believed that nothing could ever stop me. I really did." We can really learn a lot from that. No loss should ever deter you from going forward. You are the master of your destiny, and your power to succeed will come from your belief in yourself.

These pages have been focused on mentors and planning, attitude and determination, learning and growing, risk-taking, perseverance, service, developing great habits, being the best while taming the ego, building relationships and networking, developing your voice, nurturing goodness and grace, finding joy and delivering the goods, writing your own story, and so much more.

But it all boils down to the simplicity of a thought that many have attributed to Benjamin Franklin:

Never let the sun catch you sleeping.

Commit to being the very best in your chosen field of endeavor. Become the best, and then do more, give more, and be more, because you are the best. The greater the success, the greater the responsibility to others.

You must be driven, and that means that you must never allow curveballs or setbacks to stop you from pursuing your goals and your dreams. No matter the issue, you go forward and you act in the living present to take the next step and make the next move. Every day you are given 24 hours, and it is up to you to use each precious hour as best you can.

Charlie and His Lessons

I have been proud to share with you an incredibly inspirational and motivational story—that of my grandfather, Charlie, who left all the beauty of

Kyrenia in Cyprus and all the love he knew at the age of 16, and traveled in the steerage of a ship in search of a better life.

To me, Charlie's life is the stuff of which movies are made. For you, he should be a model in your own pursuit of success and a best life. Charlie Pistis is a textbook in and of himself. It was his grandfatherly mentoring that allowed me to become all that I am.

He taught me that an upbeat, positive attitude is everything, and that it is possible to fashion dreams and extract joy and purpose out of life, even if the only guidepost that one has is the need to survive—and even when the only driver in the rear view mirror is desperation. He taught me that one can build a best life out of nothing beyond the surprises that appear along the way. He taught me the value of humility and the need to keep the ego in check. He taught me the value of learning, and listening, and risking, and persevering, and working hard, and always giving more than that which is required of me.

He taught me that everyone out there—literally everyone—has something to teach me, and that I was capable of achieving whatever I chose. He liked to say that every person on the street had something to teach me and some wisdom to share.

He told me that if I could imagine it, I could be it, which is just what I have done.

He taught me that every new day fashions new opportunities. The sun rises, he'd insist, and so too do the invitations to explore new chances and possibilities. He taught me that the secret is to never stop moving and that "action is ever and always the antidote to despair."

I have memorialized a countless amount of his sayings, but I'll remind you of just these two:

"I celebrated when I was a dishwasher. All work has its dignity and its honor."

"Limits are artificial creations."

From the bottom of my heart, thank you, Charlie.

A Final "Few" Words, Inspired by Charlie

- You choose. You determine. You make it happen. In truth, this should not be a secret, but the distinct lack of faith in the principle renders it one. It is you who must discover your particular purpose and passion in life.

- Identify the mentor or mentors who will help guide and advise you along the way.

- Develop a plan of action that might include more education or training, formative jobs or steps, prospective paths to advancement, a prospective transition from employee to entrepreneur, the inevitable goal or dream, and all the connectors that tie these steps together.

- You are often met by a choice between hard and easy. Choose what is hard.

- Hard is the road less traveled, but it is the best road. It always takes you higher, so take it.

- In school, choose the most demanding professors. Always choose those who will demand your best and thus help you to grow and advance. To be challenged is to be honed and steeled for whatever the future will dish out. In the real world, after all, you will be constantly challenged.

- Maintaining a positive, upbeat and pleasant attitude is a must. If you are not in the game and rooting for yourself always, neither will those around you.

- When networking, always put those you meet and their concerns first. Know that it is in the giving that you will receive.

- When you make a connection while networking, and you feel special potential with that person, set up a follow-up breakfast or luncheon meeting on the spot.

- Building relationships is key. The more good relationships you have, the more strategic alliances you have, the more friends you have, the higher the advance and the greater the success.

- While you have every right to be proud of who and what you are, hold your pride close and share it only with those closest to you. Never lead with your ego. Never!

- As much as possible, when receiving an email or text, respond in the moment, even if you can't yet provide a full answer. Inform the sender of when you will be able to respond in full, and do that within 24 hours.

- Before you are flush with money and can market and advertise optimally, get those business cards out—in diners, at public reception areas that welcome them, on grocery store caulk boards, and at any and all events that you go to. Remember, the rule is to even keep them in the baby's diaper bag. Have the card handy always. You never know.

- As you build relationships and networks and strategic alliances, it is important to communicate regularly without advertising yourself. Informative, topical, and even inspiring newsletters or bulletins are preferred. Your communication might also be tied to a charity or community organization that you support. You can share your name, logo, and brand without advertising. But the name and the brand will stick, and you'll come to do business with many by going through the back door rather than the front.

- Devote time every day to reading, learning and expanding your mind and your horizons for your enterprise, your industry, and your world. To be the expert, "attention must be paid."

- Always do what you can to raise up those in your company or circle. In helping them to improve, you can't help but improve yourself. In lending a hand, others will reach out for yours.

- Remember that it's never possible to get everything done. The inbox is never empty. Breathe deep, relax, and know that tomorrow awaits you.

- At the end of each day, consider what mattered or was of value in it and then apply it to the next day.

The Most Important Habit of All

I have always worked to impress my superiors with my willingness to go beyond what was required, and to excel—even if it was for the sake of excellence alone, and not a promotion or a raise. Committing to excellence and to being the best for its own sake has set me free. For a best life is to live beyond the norm, the usual, or the expected.

Since that is to be you, you must start distinguishing yourself from the moment you become an aware human being. And always remember to accept criticism so that it may allow you to continue to improve, advance, and be the best that you can be.

Ready, Set…Give Your Best!

Living your best life requires *giving your best always*. And, ultimately, you must do it with joy. As Charlie said, "I seldom met a man I didn't like, and I enjoyed every job I ever had. My positive attitude was a relentless force for good for me."

So, steady as she goes. Now it's up to you to take the next step, and the next one, and the one after that. Think of yourself as an attitude engineer. Relentlessly pursue your dream and the fulfillment of your life's passion and purpose.

This book represents me and all that I believe. Because of that, a piece of me is with you always, and, more importantly, available to you at Marc@GrandfatherLessons.com. Take what I have written in these pages, apply it all, and I can guarantee that you will have the most incredible life.

I wish you the best on your journey and hope that you share your best self with all who know you, and all who will come to know you.

We are, after all, in this together.

Index

A

Acting. *See* Action
Action, 51–68
   difficulty of, 58–59
   living with, 52–53
   utilizing time for, 63–64
   See also Passion; Principles for success
Alliances, strategic, 118–119, 123
   See also Networking
Anna. *See* Pistis, Anna
Ask the right questions, 34–36, 35–36, 39, 41–42, 65, 98, 136
   Who am I?, 35–36, 136–137
Attitude, 51–68
   is everything, 21, 51–68, 102–106, 131, 140, 141
   living with, 53–57
   maintaining positive, 51–68, 102–106, 131
   See also Passion; Principles for success
Attitude is everything, 21, 51–68, 102–106, 131, 140, 141
   See also Principles for success

B

Be awake and alive to the suffering of others, 27, 59, 62, 64–65
   See also Principles for success
Be joyful, 30–32, 62, 64–65, 131, 134
   See also Principles for success
Be resilient, persevere, and never give up on yourself, 22, 61–62, 72–79, 103–104, 133–136, 139
   See also Principles for success
Be thankful for what you have, 28–29, 61, 134
   See also Principles for success
Be your heroes, 37–38
   See also Mentors
Believe in yourself always, 29–30, 135–136
   See also Principles for success
Bezos, Jeff, 91–93
Buffet, Warren, 89, 93-95

C

Charlie, 1–3
   Cyprus, 3–10
   Downtown Angler's Club, 18–19
   Fraunces Tavern, 18–19
   London, 11
   New York, 11–19
   Pistis, Anna, 12–14, 20
   Principles for sSuccess, 2-3, 20–32, 137–141
   West Side Tennis Club, 17–18

What would Charlie say?, 37, 49, 67, 95-96, 111, 126-127, 139-141
Zeta Psi, 15-16
Churchill, Winston, 62, 66, 77, 105
Clubhouse, 118
Communication
 skills, 80-81, 132-133
 technology, 79, 108-110
 See also Networking
Connections, productive, 118-119
 See also Networking
Constant Contact, 125
Contact management, 125-126, 132
 See also Networking
Corley, Thomas, 74
Coughlin, Tom, 95
Cyprus, Kyrenia, 4-6, 8, 9, 13-14

D
Downtown Angler's Club, 18-19

E
Emerson, Ralph Waldo, 42, 85-86
Everyone you pass in life has something to teach you, 23, 108-110, 113-127, 140-141
 See also Principles for success

F
Fraunces Tavern, 18-19
Fulghum, Robert, 3

G
Gates, Bill, 78, 89-90
Gignac, Robert, 78
Gretzky, Wayne, 95

H
Humility. *See* Remain humble always

J
Jobs, Steve, 86-88
Joyfulness, 30-32, 62, 64-65, 131, 134
 See also Principles for success

K
Kennedy, John Fitzgerald, 38, 40
Kennedy, Robert F., 95
Kyrenia, Cyprus, 4-6, 8, 9, 13-14

L
Lajoie, Nadine, 78-79
Lincoln, Abraham, 82-83, 135
LinkedIn, 118
Living purposefully, 38-40
Long, Yvette, 78
Look for what others don't see, 26-27, 60
 See also Principles for success

M
Mail Chimp, 125
Maslow, Abraham, 36, 42
Mentors, 37-38, 46-48, 115-117, 139

N
Networking, 113-127, 131-132, 139, 140-141

communication skills, 80–81, 132–133
database management, 124–126, 132
mentors, 115–117, 139
productive connections, 118–119
strategic alliances, 118–119, 123
Never stop moving in the directions of your dreams, 24–25, 33–49, 61–62
See also Principles for success
No one ever does it alone, 23–24, 37–38, 46–48, 61, 113–127
See also Principles for success

P

Passion, 33–49
ask the right questions, 34–36, 39, 41, 42
be your heroes, 37–38
as a force in life, 41–46
living purposefully, 38–40
mentors, 37–38, 46–48
self-actualization, 36–37
Seuss, Dr., 38–39, 45
Perserverance, 22, 61–62, 72–79, 103–104, 133–136, 139
Phipps, Wintley, 37–38
Pistis, Anna, 12–14, 20
Pistis, Haralambos Georgiou, 1, 3, 129
See also Charlie
Primary principles, 129–130
See also Principles for success
Principles for success
attitude is everything, 21, 51–68, 102–106, 131, 140, 141

be awake and alive to the suffering of others, 27, 59, 62, 64–65
be joyful, 30–32, 62, 64–65, 131, 134
be resilient, persevere, and never give up on yourself, 22, 61–62, 72–79, 103–104, 133–136, 139
be thankful for what you have, 28–29, 61, 134
believe in yourself always, 29–30, 135–136
everyone you pass in life has something to teach you, 23, 108–110, 113–127, 140–141
look for what others don't see, 26–27, 60
never stop moving in the directions of your dreams, 24–25, 33–49, 61–62
no one ever does it alone, 23–24, 37–38, 46–48, 61, 113–127
primary principles, 129–130
remain humble always, 25–26, 59, 140
take the mighty risk, 21–22, 33, 45, 95, 110–111
there are no limits and no ends, 29, 129, 133, 137–139
to work is to survive and that is not enough, 27–28, 33–49, 60, 77
you must go the extra mile, 25, 104, 106–108, 133
Purpose, 33–49
ask the right questions, 34–36, 39, 41, 42

be your heroes, 37–38
as a force in life, 41–46
living purposefully, 38–40
mentors, 37–38, 46–48
self-actualization, 36–37
Seuss, Dr., 38–39, 45

R

Remain humble always, 25–26, 51–68, 59, 140
  See also Principles for success
Resilience, 22, 61–62, 72–79, 103–104, 133–136, 139
Rilke, Rainer Maria, 67–68
Risk. See Take the mighty risk
Rodgers, Fred, 134

S

Self-actualization, 36–37
Seuss, Dr., 38–39, 45, 72, 136
Shell, Richard, 34, 35–36, 97
Singer, David, 76–77
Social Media, 126
Spillane, Phil, 78
Strategic alliances, 118–119, 123
  See also Networking
Success
  habits found in achieving, 74–76, 141–142
  nature of, 69–96
  personal profiles of, 82–95
  positive attitude in, 51–68, 102–106, 131
  principles for, 20–32
  tips, 55–57, 79–81, 103–105, 122–123, 131–133
  utilizing technology in, 108–110

utilizing time in, 98–102

T

Take the mighty risk, 21–22, 33, 45, 95, 110–111
  See also Principles for success
Taylor, Fredrick, 101, 102
Technology, 79, 108–110
There are no limits and no ends, 29, 129, 133, 137–139
  See also Principles for success
Thoreau, Henry David, 35, 83–84, 136
Time, 63–64, 98–102, 132
Tips, success, 55–57, 79–81, 103–105, 122–123, 131–133
To work is to survive and that is not enough, 27–28, 33–49, 60, 77
  See also Principles for success

W

West Side Tennis Club, 17–18
What would Charlie say?, 37, 49, 67, 95–96, 111, 128, 139–141
  See also Principles for success
Who am I?, 35–36, 136–137

Y

You must go the extra mile, 25, 104, 106–108, 133
  See also Principles for success

Z

Zeta Psi, 15–16

Credits

Editor: Michael Roney/Highpoint Life

Cover design: Julia McMinn Evans

Interior book design: Sarah M. Clarehart

Copyeditor and Proofreader: Maya R. Ziobro

Indexer: Karl Ackley

Special thanks to Satiama Writers Resource

www.grandfatherlessons.com

www.ingramcontent.com/pod-product-compliance
Lightning Source LLC
Chambersburg PA
CBHW071313110426
42743CB00042B/1496